Building a Multimedia Presence on the World Wide Web

Bohdan O. Szuprowicz

Computer Technology Research Corp.
6 North Atlantic Wharf, Charleston, South Carolina 29401 U.S.A.
Telephone: (803) 853-6460 • Fax: (803) 853-7210
E-mail: reports@ctrcorp.com

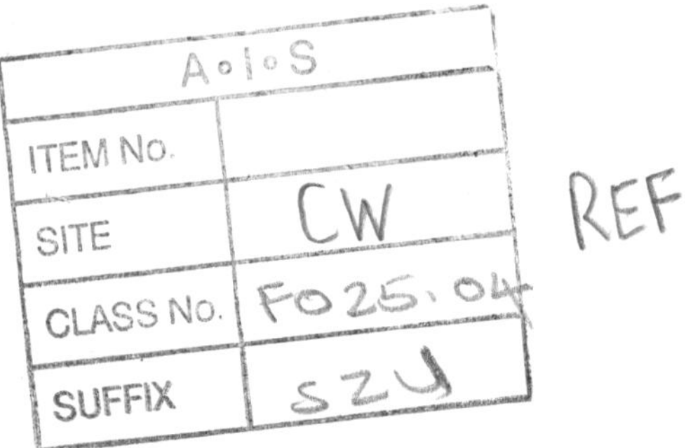

Building a Multimedia Presence on the World Wide Web

First Edition - 1996

ISBN 1-56607-962-4

Published by Computer Technology Research Corp., Charleston, South Carolina U.S.A.

Library of Congress Cataloging-in-Publication Data

Szuprowicz, Bohdan O.
Building a multimedia presence on the World Wide Web / Bohdan O. Szuprowicz. -- 1st ed.
p. cm.
ISBN 1-56607-962-4
1. World Wide Web (Information systems). I. Title.
TK5105.888.S98 1996
025.04--dc20 95-43371
CIP

BUILDING A MULTIMEDIA PRESENCE ON THE WORLD WIDE WEB

TABLE OF CONTENTS

LIST OF FIGURES

LIST OF TABLES

Introduction

This report provides an overview of the World Wide Web (the Web), and explains how to establish a Web presence and design superior Web pages using multimedia elements.

The first section of this report discusses the Internet environment and explains the Web as the multimedia aspect of the Internet. It also discusses the Web's limited ability to transmit multimedia content to the users due to high-bandwidth requirements not always available to the average Internet user.

The second section deals with the reality of corporate Web presence development and operation. It describes the different types of Web sites and presentations, Web server development, operational strategies, and the issues involved with multimedia access to the Web sites by Internet users.

The last section covers the practical aspects of Web home page and site development. It discusses numerous types of tools for providing access to the Web, development and search tools, agents and avatars, creation of pages using Hypertext Markup Language (HTML), use of various Web page editors, and the various Web development and presentation services available to corporate sponsors.

The report consists of 10 chapters:

1) Executive Summary
2) Anatomy of the Web
3) Multimedia Strategies for the Web
4) Multimedia Access to the Web
5) Multimedia Web Browsers

6) Multimedia Agents on the Web
7) Creating a Multimedia Presence on the Web
8) Web Multimedia Development Tools
9) Web Development and Presentation Services
10) Conclusions

Chapter 1, The Executive Summary, focuses on important issues information systems (IS) managers should remember when designing, deploying, and maintaining a corporate Web presence. As such, it will help in understanding the many technical and operational problems likely to occur when a corporate Web presence is contemplated.

The Web is often referred to as the multimedia aspect of the Internet and is analyzed in Chapter 2. It outlines the relative size of the Web compared with the overall Internet infrastructure, and describes the multimedia characteristics that distinguish the Web from other Internet protocols and resources. The chapter also covers the different types of multimedia applications found on the Web. In addition, this section discusses the factors that make a Web site stand out among competing sites, and identifies the sources of additional information about Web home page design and Web sites judged to be the best in the world.

One of the most important discussions of corporate Web presence is covered in Chapter 3. It explains whether a corporation must have a Web presence, and how it can justify the design, deployment, and maintenance costs. The chapter also covers the various alternatives for establishing a Web presence – comparing the renting of space on a Web server to the development of a corporate Web server with direct access to the Internet. The associated issues of security, development of firewalls, and encryption procedures in Web-related traffic also are discussed in detail in this chapter.

In Chapter 4, the report provides a detailed discussion of the problems associated with establishing multimedia access to the Web. It underscores the issue of required bandwidth to provide an acceptable multimedia access to the Web by end-users and Web page developers. The chapter explains the various connectivity options available through Internet Service Providers (ISPs). It also shows how to evaluate the growing number of ISPs with regard to their high-speed transmission capabilities, multiple points of presence, international coverage, and Web site development assistance capabilities. The chapter identifies a number of sources and contact points that could provide information and assistance for developing a corporate Web presence program through its various logical stages.

The Web browsers, which are among the most important software tools for searching and creating a presence on the Web, are covered in detail in Chapter 5. This chapter explains the functions of a browser, its capabilities, limitations, and rapidly changing specifications. The chapter also explains how a typical Web browser handles multimedia content of Web pages. What users must do to ensure they can receive multimedia elements originally included in many Web sites and home pages is also discussed. There is a special discussion of the steps that must be taken to display graphics, audio, and video content of a Web site, and the specific viewers that must be used with Web browsers.

Chapter 6 discusses the increasing problem of searching and locating valuable materials and content on the Web. The number of Web servers is so large and is increasing so rapidly that it is impossible for a user with the most advanced browser tools to search even a small percentage of the total Web universe. The chapter discusses the efforts directed at the development of a more efficient search engine and the use of robots, agents, spiders, and avatars that can perform electronic searches continuously within very precise parameters encoded into their memories. The chapter discusses a number of multimedia-related search concepts that appear to have a potential for Web applications. A comparison of Web search products and agent technologies is also included in this chapter.

The process of creating a multimedia presence on the Web is outlined in Chapter 7. This section is targeted toward those who require more detailed information about the preparation of Web documents using HTML language. The chapter explains the basics of HTML and the way multimedia elements are handled. It also discusses the need to develop the best possible interface design for the user and the process of "storyboarding the Web" to make it possible. This chapter also covers the steps that must be taken to announce and promote a corporate presence on the Web to lure visitors to a particular Web site. The function of a "Webmaster" and the need to provide strong and well-supported leadership for successful design, development, and deployment of a Web presence is also covered.

Chapter 8 covers specific categories of Web site design and development tools that can be used by various types of multimedia Web site developers. It includes a discussion of the basic Hypertext Transport Protocol (HTTP) which is the basis of the HTML language for coding Web pages. The chapter also covers other Internet protocols such as File Transfer Protocol (FTP) and Gopher, and their potential contributions to the development of Web servers and pages. In addition, this chapter explains the concepts of HTML graphical and tag editors and HTML converters that transform existing text into HTML pages suitable for use on Web sites. The chapter compares typical Web development tool products from leading vendors and provides Uniform Resource Locator (URL) addresses for additional information about those tools. It also looks at the future tools for Web page development such as Java, BlackBird, and Virtual Reality Modeling Language (VRML), which are now being incorporated into Web design and manipulation tools.

Web development services, which can provide Web presence design, development, and maintenance for corporate clients, is discussed in Chapter 9. This chapter presents a comparison of Web development services available from telephone carriers, Internet service providers, and other Web service vendors.

Chapter 10 focuses on various trends including the development of integrated Web browsers and Web server development tools. All conclusions are geared toward handling multimedia aspects of Web presence development and networking.

The report also includes a glossary of terms pertaining to multimedia networking and the Web. It covers the terminology used by the industry insiders involved with the development of interactive multimedia communications.

Chapter 1

Executive Summary

The Internet and the Web are the global communications phenomena of the last decade of the twentieth century. These systems are growing unchecked into a worldwide movement that many economists and social scientists believe will drastically change the way business is conducted. Whether this will have such an impact is still unclear. Nevertheless, most businesses throughout the world – large and small alike – are not taking any chances and are rushing to establish a presence on the Web.

What is becoming rather obvious as time progresses, however, is that a basic Web presence is not particularly attractive or meaningful. Some observers now suggest it is better not to have a Web presence unless it is fully supported by corporate management, and designed and implemented with top-quality talent and resources.

The Global Internetworking Craze

Although the Internet as a concept is more than 25 years old, it is only during the last two years that there has been a global rush to get online. The Internet itself is truly the mother of all the networks, linking thousands of private and public networks and millions of computers. Thanks to a standard Transmission Control Protocol/Internet Protocol (TCP/IP), any computer can connect to the Internet, including personal computers (PCs), UNIX workstations, minicomputers, and mainframes running under a variety of operating systems. Although the Internet was originally based on UNIX platforms, any hardware platform can now operate on the Internet as long as it supports the TCP/IP networking protocol.

The number of Internet users is growing exponentially as measured by the numbers of individuals acquiring some form of connectivity to the system. What is not quite clear, however, is how many of the individuals with access to the Internet are actual users of its resources beyond the initial free trial period. This is an important question given that initial connectivity software is often given away free-of-charge to induce the largest possible number of people to experience the Internet.

Nevertheless, there is a growing population of corporate Internet users who are linking their global facilities across Internet networks for communications purposes. Such business users, together with merchants of various goods and services, constitute the commercial population of users on the Internet, which until recently catered to the academic, research, and government communities.

Despite rapid growth and enthusiasm of its proponents, the Internet is not without problems and growing pains. One of the major issues is lack of data transmission security, which precludes serious commercial exploitation of the Internet by banks and financial services. Another aspect of Internet security concerns the vulnerability of internal corporate local area networks (LANs) and wide area networks (WANs) to hacker attacks through their links to the Internet.

To take advantage of the Internet, corporations must design special firewalls to deny access to unauthorized outsiders and employ elaborate encryption procedures to secure corporate transmissions. Needless to say, such measures can be very costly and their implementation must be justified by the company.

When perceived as a global sales and marketing system, another problem facing the Internet is the relative low bandwidth of the connections used by the greatest number of users. These are mostly low-bandwidth telephone lines with 14.4 Kbps or at best 28.8 Kbps modems, and are unsuitable for transmission in an efficient and timely manner of interactive multimedia traffic across the Internet.

As a result, multimedia content and multimedia traffic on the Internet is concentrated on the Web servers and networks which form only a subset of all Internet networks and computers. Due to its multimedia applications, the Web is the most visible part of the Internet and is attracting the bulk of commercial interest and investment.

What Makes the Web Go 'Round

The Web is a network of computer servers of all categories that contain documents encoded with the HTML, which provides the links between Web pages wherever they exist. For example, many companies, academic institutions, government agencies, and individuals create a presence on the Web in the form of a "home page" with links to company logos, elaborate graphics, images, and audio and video clips.

The Web is estimated to include tens of thousands of such computer sites worldwide, although more than 50% of those exist in North America. The number of Web servers is growing rapidly as these Web sites are developed by individual corporations and a variety of organizations offering Web servers or Web space for rent.

These Web servers are usually UNIX workstations or powerful PCs operating in multiuser environments using special software that allows access to the Web server by a large number of simultaneous users.

Corporations and organizations that wish to establish a Web presence develop a Web home page identified by a URL address. Each URL includes an indication that it operates under the HTTP on a Web site identified by specific computer, path, and file names.

Web servers are linked with the Internet either directly or more often through Internet Service Providers (ISPs) that operate high-bandwidth links to accommodate the continuous data traffic between random users and the various home pages being searched and visited. It is important to remember that increasing use of multimedia content on Web home pages stretches the demand for bandwidth capacity. Web pages with heavy multimedia content should be based on Web servers with high-speed links to the Internet backbones because otherwise it will be too time-consuming and frustrating to access such pages.

It is also important to realize that the majority of Internet and Web users today do not have multimedia PC platforms or adequate bandwidth to effectively download multimedia content from Web sites. By the same token, Web browser tools on the market today are not all configured to handle multimedia transmissions. Thus, careful planning and analysis is required to determine the best Web server location and home page design so it can be accessed and viewed by the largest segment of the target population.

The most sensible strategy is to evaluate Web servers in operation and collect initial demographics about their use and value to their sponsors. The Web as a marketing system is in its initial stages and should be viewed as a public relations and advertising device and as a market research tool. After initial testing of a Web presence a company may find no marketing benefits, but may find it to be valuable as an internal corporate communications system.

Everything and the Kitchen Sink...

The variety of topics on the Internet in general, and on the Web in particular, are as diverse as life itself. There are thousands of Web business sites, representing dozens of industries ranging from one-person consultancies to multibillion dollar corporations.

Businesses present home pages which are supported, in many cases, by extensive background information about the company, its products and services, and in some cases, they provide online ordering facilities. The amount of business transacted online through the Web at this stage, however, is minuscule relative to any business at a major shopping mall. Although impressive growth statistics are often quoted, these are based on very small initial annual sales estimates.

Of the industries developing Web hardware and software, Internet access providers, telecommunications, and Web services are the most numerous. This is indicative of the Web itself – a complex interactive multimedia networking environment that appeals predominantly to businesses associated with information technology (IT) products or services. For many of these companies, the business consists of transmitting software files and subsequent product updates to clients. The Internet is an inexpensive transmission network designed for this purpose.

The home pages representing various businesses on the Web can range from very simple personal skills pages including a photograph of the person, to extremely elaborate corporate presentations consisting of many interrelated pages with logos, graphics, images, audio messages, and video clips. Home pages may reside on shared Web servers or on dedicated corporate host computers operated directly by the corporation.

There is another group of businesses that are natural exploiters of the Web. These types of industries include art, interactive advertising agencies, books and publications, film production and video services, graphics and special effects suppliers, law firms, magazines, multimedia content sources, music, news and information, publishing firms, technical consulting, and research.

Various service industries are also establishing Web presences, particularly where they can use the Web to provide customer services to their business clientele. These industries include airlines, agricultural services, banks and financial services, business services, health and medicine, local tourist services, personal services, real estate, and all forms of travel and transportation services. Many of these Web services operate on a business-to-business basis where the business clients are in a position to invest in suitable multimedia capable PCs and high-speed communications links.

Web presence development strategy should begin by exploring many, if not most, competitive Web sites. The problem of finding such Web pages in cyberspace is solved by connecting to Web directories and consortia, many of which are industry-specific while others are extremely comprehensive with numerous categories. Most directories include specific sections on Web business sites, while others offer extensive multimedia design and development sources and services that can be particularly useful in developing a corporate Web presence strategy and implementation program.

Deciding What to Do

Perhaps the first, and most important decision, is whether a particular company must have a presence on the Web at all. A Web site or service may not be a profitable undertaking at the outset, and perhaps will never be profitable. The results do not necessarily depend on how elaborate the home pages are and how often they are visited, but by the nature of the business and its suitability for the Web. Otherwise, a Web presence must be regarded as a public relations exercise and expenditure.

Some businesses will never be able to justify a Web presence simply because their clientele may not be computer literate or may not even care or want to own and operate a computer. It is argued, however, that sooner or later access to the Web will be available to most households through the means of interactive television (TV), electronic cybermalls, and other online services. Be that as it may, analysts now realize it will take many years before a significant percentage of the TV and cable TV population will have the means and desire to become a massive purchasing public for the Web.

Yet, businesses must acknowledge the significant potential of the Internet and the Web. As a result, most large corporations are expected to take the plunge and establish a Web presence, if only for research and promotional purposes. The issue, therefore, boils down to how to do it in the easiest and most profitable manner.

Initially perhaps, the most important step is to impress upon top management that a corporate Web presence effort should be supported to the fullest with an adequate budget and all the required resources. Because a Web presence represents a corporation to the world at large, it should be the best possible effort including top-quality skills and resources.

This applies not only to the design and development of the Web site itself, but also to timely maintenance and updating which will keep users returning to the site. If a company is not prepared to commit the required resources to the maintenance aspect, it is best not to have a Web presence at all.

Many low-budget and poorly developed Web sites include a warning to the users that the site is "under construction." This has now become such a cliché that more often than not it is assumed such Web pages have been abandoned due to lack of funding or inadequate skills and design resources.

Before developing the Web site, a thorough search of the competitive Web sites should be made to evaluate their locations, traffic intensity, and operating costs. On the basis of such competitive analysis, a decision must be made whether to have a corporate Web server linked directly to the Internet or whether to rent a Web server or share one operated by an ISP organization. At this point, an evaluation of suitable ISPs should be undertaken with a careful plan for flexible connectivity arrangements.

Significant attention must be given to protecting the internal corporate networks from unauthorized access through the Web connections. This may involve firewalls and encryption systems, each of which will mean additional expenditures, skills, and maintenance requirements. It is also important to remember in this connection that a poorly implemented and maintained security system is worse than no security system at all.

Is a Multimedia Presence on the Web Worth the Effort?

Companies are rapidly creating Web home pages containing some multimedia elements. In many cases, these are simple graphic logos or images of the executives, personnel or company locations. Actual audio and video are not as prevalent, but are increasing in number.

The objective in creating a Web presence is to find the most attractive yet practical home page design which presents a professional interface to any user who may visit it. The most important consideration with regard to the home page interface design is the intended end-user population and their capability to access and download multimedia objects.

The home page should be designed in such a way that it conveys all the intended messages and information about linkages to other pages and resources. Users must be given a choice of whether to download multimedia objects such as graphics, images, audio, and video clips. Otherwise, such multimedia objects may be impossible for many visitors to download or so frustrating in transmitting over low-bandwidth connections that users will avoid visiting the site altogether.

The recommended approach to the design of a home page is to "storyboard the Web" – creating a connectivity flow diagram by laying out all the Web page levels with multimedia objects and specific linkages between them.

The development of home pages requires the use of HTML language and creation of HTML documents. These are pages whose text is marked-up with HTML tags representing the start and end of different headings, paragraphs, images, and linkages with other pages.

Introduction of graphics, images, audio, and video clips requires external files containing such multimedia objects. These files are given specific URL addresses and can be linked to the home page with "hot spots," which may be in the form of icons, small graphics or even thumbnail images.

The use of audio and video in home pages requires such linkage anchors to specific audio or video files which can be activated for display only when a user clicks on the link and is equipped with appropriate multimedia-capable platforms. In addition, the user must be able to process the specific audio or video file formats in which the objects are encoded.

The best home page designs provide two or more alternative audio and video choices covering the most popular file formats. This is a method of ensuring the largest possible number of users will be able to view such multimedia content if they are equipped with suitable computer platforms and Web browsers configured to handle external files of this type.

Design of the most attractive Web pages does not in and of itself guarantee it will become popular or frequently visited. Sponsors of new Web pages must promote their home pages on various Web directories and user groups. In addition, many companies advertise the existence of their home pages in traditional media such as radio, TV, newspapers, and magazine advertisements.

The task of creating and maintaining a corporate Web presence must be planned, budgeted, and coordinated with full top-management support. It requires specialized leadership in the form of specialized managers known as "Webmasters."

Chapter 2

Anatomy of the Web

The Web is the multimedia aspect of the Internet and is seen as best suited for those interactive communications pertaining to electronic commerce. It consists of a community of networked resources which deliver multimedia files to users on request.

The Web was developed at the European Center for Nuclear Research (CERN), the Swiss particle physics research center in Geneva, Switzerland. It consists of documents on servers linked to each other and marked-up in HTTP format which allows text, graphics, audio, and video to be accessed on demand.

The use of the Web requires software known as a "browser." Mosaic, a popular browser, is a Windows-like interface and is credited with changing the complex UNIX command line of the Internet interface into a more user-friendly graphical user interface (GUI). *Mosaic* allows the user to browse various types of multimedia documents stored on Web servers. Because about one million copies of the original free Mosaic software were acquired by 1995, the Web is considered to be a potential medium for services such as interactive home shopping and banking.

More sophisticated commercial browsers are now available, supplied by a growing number of vendors who have improved the original Mosaic software. Some of these products include data encryption capabilities, which makes them suitable to perform credit card transactions. Most are available for Windows, X-Windows, Macintosh, and OS/2.

Such a networking environment appears to be of immense value to business as a new broadcasting, publishing, and communications network reaching millions of the largest organizations in the world and the most affluent individuals.

This new business communications environment is developing from the bottom-up because the Web client and server software is free or very inexpensive and simple to use. As a result, Internet host computers in the commercial domain continue to surge ahead at the fastest rate. It is now the largest group, having surpassed educational sites that dominated the Internet in previous years. Web registered host computers are now the most numerous commercial sites on the Internet.

Multimedia Content on the Internet

Until the advent of the multimedia-related Web on the Internet, the predominant and universal application was E-mail. The Web, however, is much more appealing because it can handle text, sounds, graphics, and video and provides easy hypertext linking of resources on practically all the platforms that are connected to the Internet.

The Web provides access to graphics and video materials which users can navigate using hypermedia documents. Most recently a 3-D WebSpace browser was introduced by Silicon Graphics, Inc. (SGI) which dramatically changes the experience of "surfing" the Web. It allows spinning, rotation, and walk-through simulations based on virtual reality modeling language (VRML), which make the Web even more attractive for conducting electronic commerce. Due to the uneven bandwidth of Internet infrastructure, the retrieval of multimedia data is often frustrating and unpredictable. Special services are being designed to alleviate those problems.

The Web is an excellent means of selling to someone who is familiar with electronic commerce and has a computer with a modem, but it is useless in developing new business comparable to display advertising in trade magazines or national newspapers. Many businesses find they must add Web addresses to conventional advertising and team with other Web companies cross-linking to each other's sites. In the retail sector, the idea is to set-up a storefront in a cybermall, which itself is being promoted through traditional forms of advertising, by the operator. It may be that the best way to acquire new business through the Internet is to join a specialized cybermall that will be promoted by the operators or some form of the Web Yellow Pages.

The Web is an interactive multimedia communications resource to be considered within the overall program of a corporation, but the Web should not be viewed as a ready-built alternative for a competitive interactive multimedia communications system. Rather, it is a component of the information super-highway with multimedia transmission facilities, currently lacking in real-time capabilities.

The mass market for multimedia on the Web is limited because individual PC owners do not connect to the Web with high-speed lines. Therefore, they are unable to obtain the multimedia effects of those sites. The best Web use is to deliver customer service to existing clients of large corporations or communicate with widely-dispersed sites of the same company. Without guaranteed fast response for videoconferencing and secure communications, even those applications are questionable.

The ANS Backbone

ANS CO+RE Systems, Inc. of Elmsford, New York, designs, develops, and operates high-performance wide area data networks for business, research, education, and government organizations; it constitutes the main backbone for Web transactions. ANS operates a nationwide 45 megabytes per second (Mbps) TCP/IP public data network and provides Internet connectivity to various access providers. The ANS backbone is actually composed of leased digital transmission lines capable of carrying data at 45 Mbps (T3) speeds. These circuits are connected into a mesh topology with packet switches or routers, located where transmission circuits intersect at major cities. These intersection points also constitute core network entrance nodes for regional and local access providers.

Figure 2.1 illustrates the basic ANS network within the United States.

Figure 2.1 The ANS Backbone in the United States

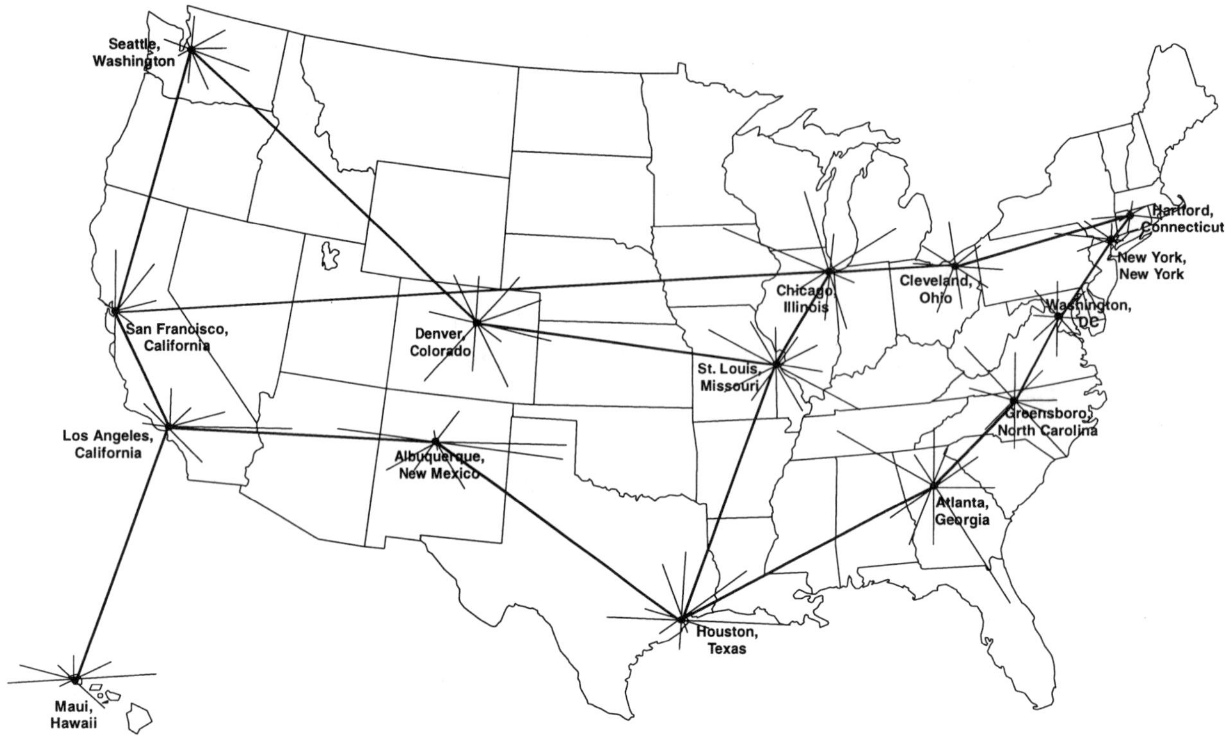

The number or users is growing rapidly and they are increasingly transmitting multimedia content (including video) which requires significantly more bandwidth capacity than text or audio content. When commercial multicasting applications are thrown into the mix, the existing pipelines are insufficient to the task unless their capacity increases faster than the multimedia traffic. Commercial multicasting on the Internet is the major interest of corporations who see it as a low-cost means of promoting and advertising their products and services. There will be more, rather than less, of such activities.

The extent of the effect that the increasing multimedia traffic will have on Internet activity is still not clear because new networks being linked to the Internet can only be expected to increase both in bandwidth and users. This will only further aggravate the traffic issues. If serious slowdowns occur today, there is an urgent need to improve the backbone infrastructure with higher capacity fiberoptic links, and larger and more powerful switches and routers.

On Tuesday, September 5, 1995, during the midday hours, an Internet traffic overload slowed its operations to unprecedented and unacceptable levels. Some users trying to access the Web reported delays of more than 40 minutes to get into some sites. In still other cases, connections were not established despite lengthy waits. In other instances, data was lost in cyberspace. It is becoming critically important to determine how increasing traffic on some Web sites slows access and delivery of the messages.

A massive slowdown is inevitable as long as users are provided increasingly faster links to the Internet, and as more bandwidth-hungry multimedia traffic is generated by commercial Web transmissions with complex graphics and video content.

How Big Is the Web?

By January 1995, 22,000 commercial sites appeared on the Internet, listing products, prices, data, and advertisements about companies large and small.

No one knows exactly how large the Web actually is at any particular point in time because of the rapid growth in Web servers, sites, and home pages. According to Forrester Research, however, the number of online users dialing directly into the Web was estimated at more than 3 million in early 1995. This number is expected to increase to 10 million users sometime between 1997 and 1998, and to reach an estimated 22 million by the year 2000 (see Figure 2.2).

Figure 2.2 Growth in Web Users to the Year 2000

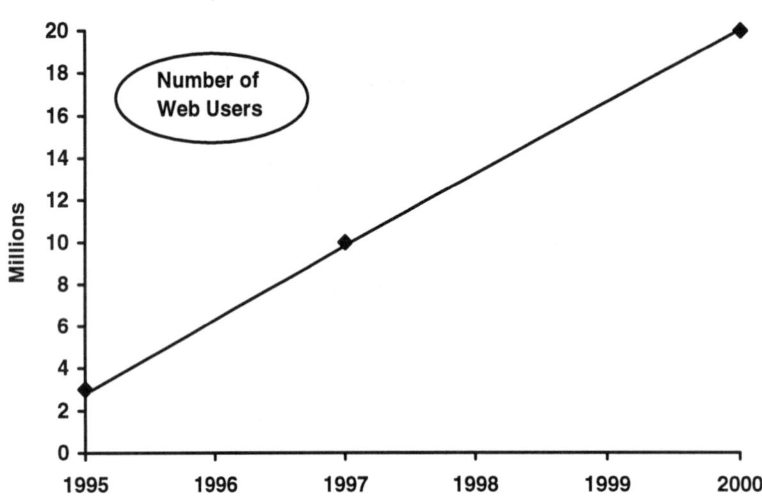

The developers of the Web at CERN are trying to keep track of new Web servers by registration. Unfortunately, registration is not strictly enforced and depends on a Web site owners or creators to voluntarily send E-mail messages to CERN describing their Web sites. While the list developed at CERN is only partial, it is categorized by continents, countries, and states and provides a good idea of Web sites in a particular region or country of the world. This Web site list can be accessed at:

http://info.cern.ch/hypertex/DataSources/WWW/Servers.html.

How Fast Is It Growing?

Jupiter Communications predicted that the 1.5 million home Web subscribers in 1995 will skyrocket to more than 40 million by 1999, creating a meaningful advertising base to be targeted by businesses of all categories.

According to the Internet Society (ISOC), the Web grew twenty-fold since 1988. During the 18 months ending in mid-1995, users created more than 3 million multimedia pages of information, advertising, and entertainment.

Another way of looking at the growth of the Web is to evaluate its electronic commerce impact. A new report on Electronic Commerce through CD-ROM Catalogs, Web Storefronts, and Internet Malls has been conducted by INPUT of Mountain View, California This report suggests the value of goods and services sold through those media will increase from an estimated $700 million in 1995, to $230 billion by the year 2000.

This growth implies an incredible compound annual growth rate of more than 200% and assumes buyer confidence will develop in network security, transaction privacy, and trading partner authentication. The report concludes that although a large proportion of current electronic sales occur through the shopping services of online businesses such as America Online (AOL), CompuServe, and Prodigy, most of the projected growth will take place as a result of new services being developed on the Web.

Hyperlinks and Hypermedia

Web documents, or home pages, are cross-linked to one another with words, phrases or images. These are the "hyperlinks" and they form the basis of the Web concept itself. Browser tools allow users to traverse those links by clicking on these items. Hyperlinks enable the pursuit of information that is of most interest at a particular moment, and make analysis of documents much more effective.

Hyperlinks are the opposite of linear links where the documents or pages follow one another in sequence without alternate paths being available. Hypertext actually means text with links, while hypermedia sometimes is used to define documents with images, graphics, and video also linked through those items. Hyperlinks is a more generic definition of those links for any multimedia content.

In effect, hyperlinks provide numerous paths through a body of information and images. In the Web environment, hyperlinks perform the function of providing a variety of media elements to enhance a single document producing a hypermedia product. The concept of hyperlinks and hypermedia is illustrated in Figure 2.3.

Figure 2.3 The Concept of Hyperlinks

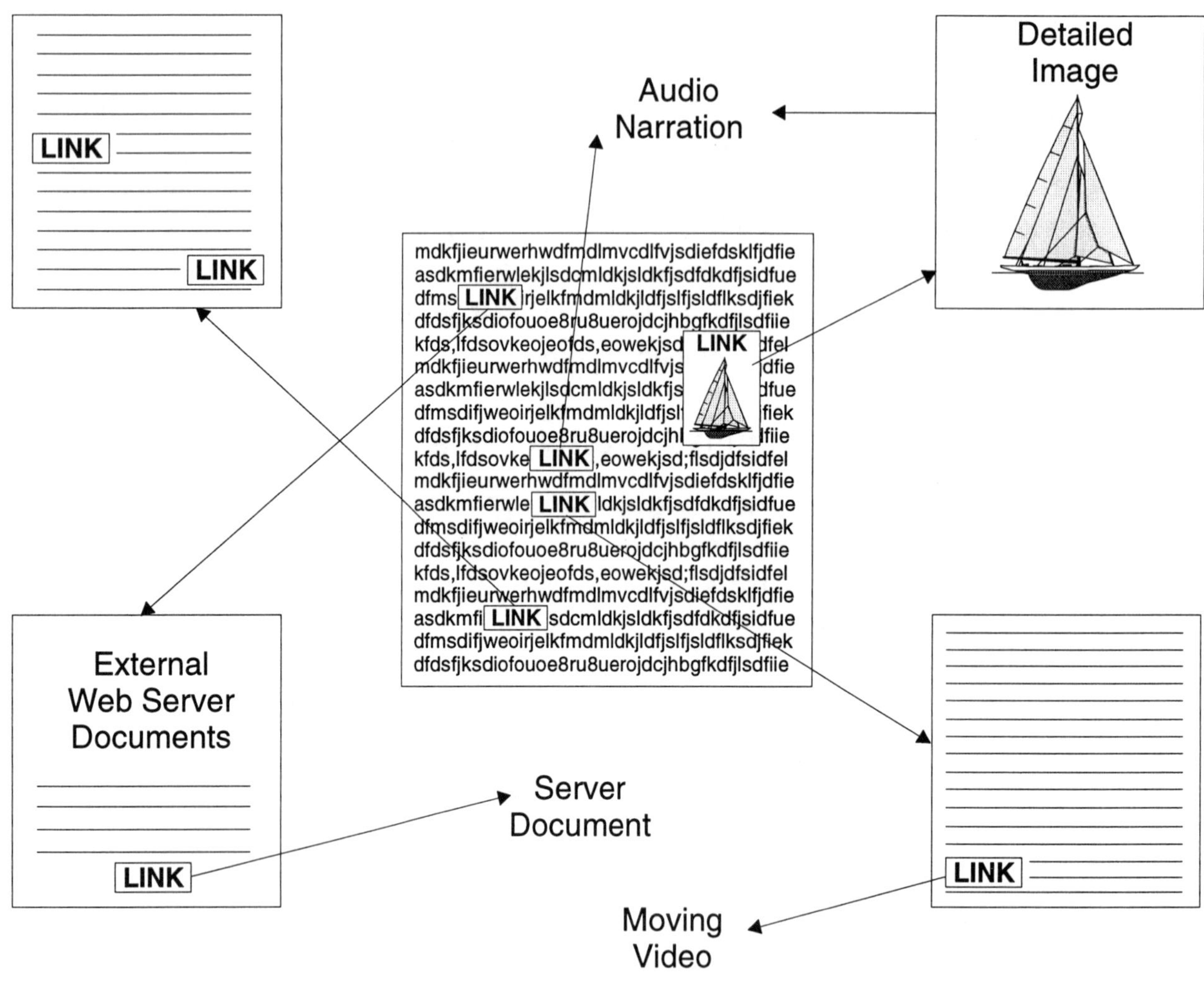

Images on the Web

Images on the Web often contain a variety of items, each of which represents some information content. Such images can be made into hyperlinked zones and become clickable images. They are created by defining specific zones of the overall image using squares, circles or polygons around specific items in the image. The coordinates of such clickable zones are associated with specific URLs in a special file known as an "imagemap."

Web pages are not considered complete without at least one image. The addition of images makes Web pages comparable to real books or magazines. Images can be inserted on the page itself or hyperlinks can be clicked on to display external files of images, sound, and movies, as necessary.

Many users do not have links to the Web with sufficient bandwidth to make downloading of images and video a practical procedure. Users with slow connections may have to wait for a significant amount of time to download images. Therefore, most pages are designed in such a way that when the connection is relatively slow, the user can choose to obtain the text without the images. In some cases, icons and small generic graphics are transmitted in the first instance indicating the existence of an image and providing an alternative to download it at a later time if required.

Uniform Resource Locator

The URL is the specific address of a document on the Internet and describes virtually any file regardless of the protocol required to reach and read it. URL makes it possible to access information stored on the Internet under several systems, each of which has developed its own specific set of software commands and communications protocols. The URL is a standard method of indicating a particular site or home page on the Web or Internet. The URL can reference any type of document on the Internet including text, graphics, audio or video and this setup allows the Web to extend into multimedia content manipulation.

The URL permits a user using a browser to retrieve information from a specific Web server. The specific URL tells the browser how to get in touch with the specific Web server, informs the server to perform a retrieval function to find the information in a specific file, and directs the browser where to transmit the results. The process is invisible to the user, who is only required to know the URL and type it into the appropriate window or click on a particular link representing that URL.

A typical URL consists of three basic components and each part must be present for the client program to contact the proper Web server addressed by the URL. These three components include the protocol statement, the Web server "home" of the document and the full path name of the file being accessed in that server.

The protocol part of the URL represents the various tools or segments of the Internet including the Web, which is identified with the letters http:// that stand for Hypertext Transport Protocol and the HTML documents normally associated with the Web. Other Internet protocols also accessible from Web clients and servers include Gopher (gopher://), File Transfer Protocol (ftp://),

Telnet (telnet://), and USENET (news:), but these are primarily protocols for handling text and data rather than multimedia content.

The second part on a typical URL identifies the Web server that holds the information being accessed, and includes all the acronyms to the first single slash, for example: http://www.name.com.ext.55/. In this case, "www" indicates the name of the Web server which is located at "name" that can identify a specific company or person which is a "com" or commercial connection. The "ext" may further identify an extension for a particular client, while the number "55" is optional and indicates a specific port other than the default port 80 that http normally connects.

The third mandatory component of a URL is the full path name of the file being accessed. This may include the document name and the names of all the directories in which the document resides. Using the previous example, http://www.name.com.ext.55/dir/file.html would indicate the "file" in question is located in a "dir" directory and is written in ".html" hypertext language. Ordinary text files may have extensions such as ".txt," while graphic files may be designated by ".gif" or ".jpg"

It is mandatory that URLs are entered precisely as they are given. This includes the single or double slashes, specific upper and lower case letters, numbers, and symbols such as hyphens and underscores. If any URL is not entered precisely, the Web client will indicate an error because it will not be able to access the information requested by the user.

On the other hand, once the structure of the URL is analyzed and understood, it becomes a useful guide to the type of information it may represent, where that information is located, and under what file name it is stored. In effect, a URL becomes an address comparable in structure to a post office box with the name of a country, city, and zip code.

What Is a Web Server?

A Web server is simply a networked multiuser computer on which the HTML and graphic files are stored under the TCP/IP protocol, with a connection to the Internet. The Web server can run under any operating system (OS) including UNIX variants, Windows NT or a Macintosh OS.

Within the Internet environment, there are 40,000 Web servers, each of which provides access to interactive multimedia databases with hyperlinks to other servers. A Web server gives a corporate owner an opportunity to present its products and services, and provides a means of interactive communications with clients and business partners. Considering worldwide coverage, the cost of access and maintenance of a Web server is not considered unreasonable. Because of these potential benefits and global exposure, the growth in Web servers is even faster than that of computers on the Internet, and is estimated to approximate 100% every 50 days.

Most Internet servers are UNIX-based systems, but they will support PC, Macintosh, and UNIX clients. Sun Microsystems, which supplied most Internet servers to scientific and educational communities during the early days of the Internet, dominates this marketplace with an estimated 56% market share according to another ISOC survey. Digital Equipment Corp. (DEC) with its very fast Alpha server platforms is considered to be the runner-up with 15% market share. Hewlett-Packard (HP) and IBM follow with 10% and 6% market shares respectively. Table 2.1 presents a summary of major Web server platform vendors.

Table 2.1 Major Web Server Platforms

Vendor	Basic Server Model	Telephone
Apple Computer	Power Macintosh	408/996-1010
Compaq Computer	Proliant Series	713/370-0670
Dell Computer	Power Edge	512/338-4400
Digital Equipment Corp.	Alpha Internet Servers	800/344-4825
Hewlett-Packard	Series E Workstations	415/857-1501
IBM	RISC System 6000	914/765-1900
Silicon Graphics	WebForce	415/960-1980
Sun Microsystems	Netra Series	415/960-1300
Tandem Computers	CyberWeb	408/285-6000

The ultimate in Web servers will be videoservers that can handle multiple data streams in addition to data and simple graphics. If the Web is going anywhere as a sales and marketing system, it must have the capability to deliver multimedia content of all types including continuous video streams.

- Videoservers fall into three major categories differentiated by the number of simultaneous video streams that can be handled. The PC-based videoservers that run under Windows or disk operating system (DOS) can handle up to six simultaneous users, and for best results, use a Pentium processor or better. UNIX systems fall into the midrange videoserver category with up to eight processors and can handle up to 150 video streams. The broadcast interactive TV videoservers are much larger systems based on massively parallel processing architectures and are expected to handle from 10,000 to 100,000 video streams simultaneously.

The UNIX business videoserver is the most appropriate for use as a Web server. It can be based on high-end PCs or more likely reduced instruction set computer (RISC) workstations and is usually designed to handle between 3.5 Mbps to 5 Mbps per user in a corporate networking environment, but that capability clearly depends on the capacity of the networking infrastructure. The PC-based servers of this type can handle between six to 20 simultaneous users, while midrange systems can accommodate up to 150 simultaneous users. In addition to video streaming features, these servers are collaborative in nature with bandwidth allocation facilities and are designed to operate for five to six years. Table 2.2 presents a summary of videoserver characteristics in all three categories.

Table 2.2 Videoserver Characteristics

General Videoserver Characteristics	♦ Multitasking operating system ♦ Huge multimedia storage system ♦ Large number of simultaneous users ♦ Video management software ♦ Compression and decompression capabilities ♦ Access authorization
Business Videoserver Characteristics	♦ 3.5 Mbps to 5 Mbps bandwidth per user ♦ PC-based with six to 20 simultaneous users ♦ Midrange systems handle up to 150 simultaneous users ♦ Collaborative in nature ♦ Video streaming capabilities ♦ Bandwidth allocation facilities ♦ Relatively narrowband operation ♦ Designed for five to six years of usage ♦ Use as Web servers

	♦ Merchandising kiosk servers ♦ Corporate training on demand servers ♦ 60% of corporations do not plan videoserver use
Consumer Interactive TV Videoserver Characteristics	♦ About 15 Mbps bandwidth for broadcast quality transmissions ♦ Interactive TV and video-on-demand applications ♦ Massively parallel processor based ♦ Expected to handle 10,000-100,000 simultaneous users ♦ Set-top box user controls at the TV set ♦ Requires broadband cabling networks to the home ♦ Distributory in nature ♦ Interactive billing and demographic mechanisms ♦ Cost of $5,000 to $10,000 per user to implement ♦ Questionable return on investment of about $300 to $1,000 per year per user ♦ Home shopping applications ♦ Interactive advertising potential

Market research from Para Technology, Inc. of Bellevue, Washington, estimated 112,000 Internet servers will be sold in 1995, at an average price of $15,000. This represents a $1.7 billion market in itself, without counting the consulting and services associated with design, installation, and training expenditures involved with these projects.

The average Internet server selling price is expected to decline to about $6,000 by the year 2000, according to Para Technology estimates. As a result, the total Internet server market is expected to skyrocket, reaching about $16 billion by the end of the decade.

UNIX continues to be the major Internet server solution because this system offers all the necessary communications, integrated networking, and many application development tools. Nevertheless, IBM OS/2, Novell NetWare, Banyan VINES, and Microsoft Windows NT are all competing with UNIX as potential Internet server systems in the future.

What Is a Web Client?

A Web client is the computer platform that remotely accesses the resources of another computer which can be a Web server. Web client programs are software programs that act as an interface between the user and the Web and are also known as "browsers." Retrieving and displaying information from a Web server requires a client program such as a browser which is installed on the home or office PC.

Client software transmits a request to the Web server computer directed by the specific URL, and provides an interface between the server and the user. All servers and clients are connected by the Internet throughout the world and Web protocols are the enabling means for all clients to communicate with all servers.

The Web client software contacts a specific Web server and informs that system about specific protocols and file formats supported by the client installation. This is important when locating and transmitting multimedia content because specific clients may support only some graphic file formats such as Graphic Interchange Format (GIF), Tagged Image File Format (TIFF) or Joint Photographic Experts Group (JPEG). It is possible to overcome incompatibilities in data formats between Web servers and clients because the client and the server understand each other.

Although browsers were initially designed to interact with the Web, most are now able to operate with other Internet tools and systems including Gopher servers and FTP sites. They provide an easy-to-use interface and are responsible for popularizing the use of Internet even by people with little or no computer knowledge or background.

There are two types of browsers used to access the Web. The text only browsers transmit only words and numbers and cannot handle images or graphics. They are still of great value to Web users, particularly by clients who do not have facilities to support multimedia displays, but need to determine where multimedia materials are located on the Web. Text-only browsers are much faster and often can be used with many more types of hardware and software systems.

Graphical user interface (GUI) browsers can handle images and graphics and are often easier to learn and faster to control. The GUI browsers fall into Mosaic-based tools and custom designed browsers developed by specific Internet access providers. Web clients are available for practically every computer platform ranging from dumb terminals on mainframes running under multiple virtual storage (MVS) and virtual memory system (VMS) to Windows 3.1, Windows NT, Windows 95, OS/2, X-Windows, and even MS-DOS.

What Is a Web Site?

A Web site can be a complete Web server operated exclusively by a corporation or a specific corporate file or home page resident on a Web server operated by a third-party such as an Internet access provider.

Web sites fall into several categories mostly depending on their objectives and content. Major Web site categories of significance include business directory services, Web resources, guides and utilities of interest to all users, Web marketing and business services, and Web business-related resources.

Web sites are constantly in a state of flux. Many are in the process of being developed and, when accessed, will inform the user of that fact. Most Web sites are updated with new information and the latest data with the objective to entice the user to repeatedly visit the site. It is also important to realize that Web sites come and go, URL addresses change for a variety of reasons, and new Web sites are constantly being developed that are not yet known or listed anywhere.

Multimedia Home Pages

Web presence is usually manifested through the "home pages," representing the vendor on a typical Web server. Sites can be created internally or through an outside service with experience in setting-up multimedia home pages for Web servers.

The home page can have a number of meanings in the Web environment, but it is generally the first document that appears when a particular Web client site is accessed by a user. It is the home base for exploring the Web and can be returned to at any time when the user is lost or decides that the path taken is not producing the expected results. A client home page usually has many links and provides basic information about the topic to which it refers.

A home page can also be a Web server document representing a person, a business, a company or an organization. In these cases, the home page refers to the whole document represented by a single URL address which may consist of many actual pages or screens that can be scrolled through without the use of any hyperlinks. Such server home pages provide basic information about the business and may include links to other documents, products catalogs, corporate programs, and customer services.

Such home pages can be set-up for an individual, a small business, a company department or a whole corporation. All that is needed is the HTML software, a word processor, and a browser to open and view the created files. Some browsers provide thumbnail-size images which save bandwidth and speeds retrieval of multimedia home pages, and can be expanded to full size if needed.

The major problem of electronic commerce on the Web is getting a user to see the home page of a particular vendor. This is called "making a surfer catch the wave" because, while there are millions of Internet browsers, the bulk of all the interactivity on the Internet consists of E-mail exchanges, file transfers, and forum discussions.

As a result, it is important to design home pages to capture the attention of casual browsers. This is usually accomplished using multimedia content, entertainment values, interactivity and virtuality of presentations. Desirable characteristics of these home pages should include meaningful, informative and interesting content, visually compelling presentations positioning products in a fun way, user involvement through interactive response mechanisms and changing content providing compelling reasons for users to return. Other incentives are coupons and discounts at some future date for those who accessed the page once. Desirable characteristics of these Web presentations are summarized in Table 2.3.

Table 2.3 Desirable Characteristics of Web Home Pages

Presentation Element	Desirable Characteristics
Content	♦ Meaningful ♦ Informative ♦ Interesting
Entertainment	♦ Visually Compelling ♦ Delivers Message ♦ Positions Product ♦ Entertaining Content
Interactivity	♦ User Involvement ♦ Response Mechanism ♦ Demographic Data
Virtuality	♦ Changing Content ♦ Compelling Reasons ♦ User Returns ♦ Incentives

For delivering audio, video, and animation graphics, it is important to keep bandwidth limitations in mind. Most videos require enormous amounts of storage. Therefore, their transmission will take a long time over standard telephone lincs. For this reason, very small images are used in initial searches and most of the actual video displays are usually limited to just a few seconds.

Multimedia Pages

The multimedia aspect of Web sites is primarily the graphic content of the more developed home pages created by large corporations that perceive a potential for performing one or more corporate functions on the Web. Looking at the top 25 site according to *Interactive Age* magazine, most are extremely colorful, consisting of graphics and various fonts with hot buttons in the form of labels of sensitive areas of the overall image.

Although some of the best home pages are considered to be work of art, the corporations creating these pages must remember how users will access their Web sites. Home pages with heavy multimedia content even without audio or video materials take a long time to download, and can be frustrating to view. Companies that want to get the attention of the user majority must design their home pages in a way that attracts attention with some multimedia elements and color, but is simple enough to provide reasonable retrieval time.

To what extent multimedia is used in Web sites also depends on the design of the specific Web servers. Specialized multimedia videoservers can clearly perform better and serve more users simultaneously with multimedia home pages. On the other hand, these are equally limited by the ultimate bandwidth of the desktop at which the home pages are being received.

Personal Pages

Personal home pages are a new trend on the Internet, providing personal and professional resumes about a person. These personal home pages usually include photographs of the author and provide links to inform the reader about specific interests and capabilities of the person.

Most personal home pages include full contact information and are promotional advertisements of the person in question. Some authors are small business people or consultants using the Web as a means to bring their skills to the attention of potential clients. This is particularly true in the case of computer-related skills.

Individuals are creating personal Web home pages which are also collections of information and clips on favorite TV shows, movies or musical groups and performers including singers and musicians. These Web sites could be valuable collections of such items for those who have similar preferences in the entertainment productions.

Unofficial Home Pages

Unofficial home pages are commercial Web sites that promote products or services without being sponsored by that company or organization. These pages may include lists of products, images of product uses, ideas for projects using such products, and history of product development. Lego Systems toy building blocks, Elvis Presley themes, tennis, basketball, and other sports topics and products are typical subjects of those unofficial Web sites.

Many sites are completely unauthorized by the owners of the products, raising issues about violation of corporate trademarks and logos. By the same token, such sites usually contain disclaimers which indicate they are not sponsored by the product manufacturing company. These usually include the words "official" or "unofficial" to avoid confusion. When logos are used, these are annotated as registered trademarks. Some confusion may result in cases where official and unofficial Web sites exist side-by-side.

Some companies have taken legal action against unofficial sites, but others are flattered their products are being promoted by third-parties and do not threaten the private promoters. Many product or idea boosters see themselves acting in a manner similar to fan clubs or user groups providing free publicity to a corporation, but the company usually has no control over the situation.

Corporate Communications

Many initial Web sites are actually electronic corporate communications statements as companies design their presence in several phases. The objective of the initial phase is usually to establish a presence by creating a Web home page that provides basic company and service information. As companies become familiar with their Web sites, they will introduce some interactivity and transactional activity which enables users to purchase company products and services directly from the Web site. Press releases, company product announcements, outlet locations, customer service information, and financial results are typical items of communications made available through Web home pages.

Computer Hardware and Software

Computer company Web sites are among the best because these organizations understand the potential of the Web as a promotional and marketing tool and have the skills to become early adopters of this technology. This does not necessarily mean the artistic and aesthetic value of their Web pages is in the award-winning category, however. Computer companies on the Web are aware of the rapid pace of product innovation in this industry and they focus on creating an impression of being up-to-date and providing customer services.

Computer companies have an advantage on the Web because they can provide actual software updates, demonstrations and new products that can be downloaded by the user. Most provide corporate financial information, annual reports, press releases, and descriptions of their business operations and research programs.

Technical support of those firms often takes the form of Frequently Asked Questions (FAQs), forums, newsgroups, databases of end-users, and interaction through E-mail in answering specific customer questions. As time progresses, these Web services are likely to include more multimedia content including audio and video clips to demonstrate product use and installation – particularly in cases where complex industrial equipment is involved. Table 2.4 provides a list of URLs of major computer companies.

Table 2.4 Major Computer Companies on the Web

Company Name	URL of Their Web Site
Apple Computer	http://www.apple.com
AT&T Global Information Solutions	http://www.attgis.com
Compaq Computer	http://www.compaq.com
Data General, Inc.	http://www.dg.com
Dell Computer	http://www.dell.com
Digital Equipment Corp.	http://www.dec.com
Hewlett-Packard	http://www.hp.com
IBM Corp.	http://www.ibm.com
NEC Corp.	http://www.nec.com
Power Computing	http://www.powercc.com
Silicon Graphics	http://www.sgi.com
Sun Microsystems	http://www.sun.com
Tandem Computers	http://www.tandem.com
Toshiba America	http://www.tais.com
Zenith Data Systems	http://www.zds.com

Interactive Advertising

According to a recent study by Forrester Research, Inc., the main revenue source for content providers on the Web will be advertising rather than Internet access providers. Advertising will account for the largest share of all Internet revenues in the future, growing rapidly from an estimated $37 million in 1995, to $2.6 billion in the year 2000. The study bases its estimates on the assumption that online consumers on the Internet will increase from 10 million in 1995, to about 29 million in 2000. This growth will provide an increasing critical mass with very attractive demographics that will greatly appeal to the advertisers on the Web. By comparison, revenues of Internet access providers already running at about $55 million in 1995, will increase only slightly to $100 million by the year 2000.

In theory, the low cost of advertising on the Web makes it an attractive medium. The Chiat/Day advertising agency which set-up Web sites for several clients estimates the costs of these to range from $15,000 to $150,000, which is only a fraction of what major advertisers spend on TV advertising. Nevertheless, the demographics of the Web population are still unclear beyond the fact that approximately 90% of all Internet surfers are males between 18 to 34 years old. By comparison, much of the consumer advertising is targeted at women. As time progresses, more women, teenagers, and senior citizens are expected to go online.

The current issue between advertisers and traditional Internet users is the need for bandwidth to access Web advertisements. Unless a user is connected through a 56 Kbps or T-1 line to the Web, downloading many of the Web home pages with graphics and videos can be very frustrating to all users on the Internet.

Table 2.5 Representative Interactive Advertising Web Sites

Agency	Description	URL
Apollo Advertising	Apollo Directory is an advertising search engine for the Web	http://apolo.co.uk/
Chiat/Day	An idea factory for creating and promoting brands on the Web	http://.www.chiatday.com/web
DDB Needham Interactive Communications	Presents online advertising samples and storyboards	http://www.ddbniac.com
Electric Press	Online brochure presenting services for interactive marketing	http://www.elpress.com/homepate.html
Modem Media	Interactive marketing agency services	http://www.modemmedia.com
Online Ad Agency	Marketing services for the Web including home page design	http://www.mediaworks.com
Online Classifieds	Web site for placing personal classified ads	http://mmink.cts.com/classifieds/classifieds.html
Poppe Tyson	Selection of online advertisements for high-tech companies	http://www.poppe.com

Agency	Description	URL
Virtual Advertising	Multimedia Web online advertising agency	http://www.halcyon.com/zz/top.html

Electronic Malls

On the Web, merchants can set-up electronic storefronts providing several layers of marketing materials that can interactively answer most questions asked by prospective customers. Users can define their own path of information retrieval which can include press releases, technical manuals, graphics, animation, voice comments and video. The problem is that not all users have PCs or network connectivity adequate to effectively transmit multimedia materials.

Business managers and owners who want to promote their products or services on the Internet can design the marketing pages themselves or hire an expert consulting firm to do it for them. In either case, it is a matter of setting-up a Web server, which becomes the virtual storefront of the company. This can be done on the Internet and on commercial online services. The advantage to the Web is Internet users only pay for access and not for connect time. As a result, they are likely to spend more time "surfing the 'net" and there is a better chance of finding and receiving promotion of a particular merchant.

Electronic malls or cybermalls are simulations of a shopping mall with various storefronts. Merchants can rent a storefront in such a cybermall and need not worry about the Web server design, but only about their own home page presentations. Electronic Mall on CompuServe online service, which started in 1985, is the oldest. Among its 150 electronic storefronts it includes companies such as J.C. Penney, Sears Roebuck, Land's End, Brooks Brothers, Metropolitan Museum of Art, 800-Flowers, and many others.

MarketplaceMCI is the latest and largest cybermall, announced by MCI Communications in early 1995. The long-distance telephone carrier offers MarketplaceMCI as a secure Internet shopping environment combining all the required elements into a specialized service, which is appealing to *Fortune* 1000 companies. Fourteen consumer and business companies have already opened their storefronts in that cybermall and more are ready to follow. MarketplaceMCI handles the development and maintenance of the Web servers for each storefront for which companies pay anywhere from $25,000 to $100,000 depending on complexity of the installation. In addition, store owners pay monthly rents ranging from $2,000 to $10,000 and transaction fees. The MarketplaceMCI features toll-free 800 user access and electronic shopping baskets into which purchases can be accumulated from several stores and multimedia news and other services. The MarketplaceMCI is accessible through MCI home page at **http://www.internetMCI.com**.

Electronic Business Co-op is a new organization created to address purchasing security on the Internet. It is being done by the development of encryption capable Web browsers. Those browsers allow purchasers to use credit cards in transactions which then go through a Tandem WebServer and are passed on to Checkfree network for credit approval. The co-op is an organization set-up for this purpose by Checkfree, Spyglass, V-One, and Tandem Computers.

Those who do not have the capabilities of creating a storefront can turn to multimedia developers or to Interactive Merchants Association (IMA), which has been set-up as a clearinghouse collecting home-shopping content for cybermalls. IMA has been organized by Micromall, Inc., a subsidiary of Microware Systems, to develop operating systems for set-top boxes in collaboration with DEC. IMA charges between $60,000 to $100,000 to create a store for a client and also takes negotiated percentage of sales after it places the store in a cybermall. Land's End is among the first retailers to sign-on with this organization.

Table 2.6 Representative Cybermalls on the Web

Name of Project	Description	URL
BizNet	Includes shopping center with a bank, restaurant, shops, bookstore, and apartment information	http://128.173.138/shopping.html
Commerce Net	Not-for-profit interbusiness communications sponsored by Apple, Hewlett-Packard, Intel, and National Semiconductor	http://www.commerce.net
Downtown Anywhere	Virtual city where users can sell and buy merchandise such as books, software, video games, videos, music, and services	http://www.awa.com/
Dream Shop	Storefronts aimed at upscale clientele	http://www.pathfinder.com/@@9bt0auckugEAQPAm/DreamShop/
Empire Mall	Features a wide variety of service-oriented businesses	http://empire.na.com

Name of Project	Description	URL
Imall	Numerous virtual storefronts including many business types such as computer technology stores; provides secure transactions	http://www.imall.com/homepage.html
Marketplace MCI	Largest and latest cybermall with secure Internet shopping; targets *Fortune* 1,000 firms; develops storefronts at $25,000 to $100,000; charges monthly rents $2,000 to $10,000 and transaction fees; also offers electronic baskets and toll-free access 800 numbers	http://www.internetmci.com
Shopping IN	A Web department store selling clothing, jewelry, and other products; available in low- and high-bandwidth versions with inline images on request	http://www.onramp.net/shopping_in/index.html
Worldwide Marketplace	A virtual shopping mall including retail, travel, training, and consulting	http://www.cygnus.nb.ca/

Low-Cost Publishing

A number of publishers of newspapers, magazines, and books have developed Web sites of their publications which operate as online news services. These sites include newswire-like pages with breaking news available on the Web as soon as they are entered into the electronic system – usually well before the actual publication reaches the newsstands. Many sites include full-color comic sections and other images, artwork, and photographs.

The objective of these Web sites is to keep readers coming back by constantly providing fresh and useful content. Readers can find a wide range of books, magazines ranging from creative writing to Internet-specific publications.

Typical of this type of Web site is the Pathfinder from Time Warner, Inc., which combines news, analysis, entertainment, and sports publications access on its home page. The Pathfinder site includes magazines such as *Time*, *Money*, *People*, *Sports Illustrated*, *Entertainment Weekly*, and *Vibe*. It is among the most overwhelming home pages on the Web and provides additional special-interest forums related to these popular publications.

Among the best of this Web site genre is the Mercury Center, based on the full edition of *San Jose Mercury News,* which is sorted by sections. A special search feature provides customized searching of classified ads and newswires such as lists of breaking news headlines and story summaries. This simplifies the process of monitoring development on a continuous basis.

A special information service from Individual, Inc. provides clippings from more than 500 publications with subject categories divided into 19 groups, each with several levels of detail. Although primarily text-based, it is a comprehensive service that provides rapid access to specific types of news of interest to the user. Unquestionably, this service will develop more graphic and multimedia content as it competes with other publishing Web sites of this category.

One of the largest alliances formed between a networking service and a news media organization is the agreement between MCI Communications and Rupert Murdoch's The News Corp., Ltd. The two companies are each investing $200 million to create a joint venture for delivering electronic news, education, and entertainment to consumers and businesses on a worldwide basis. This presents very large potential for publishing on the Web because The News Corp. conglomerate publishes 130 newspapers including *The New York Post* and *TV Guide,* and owns 20th Century Fox movie studios and the Fox Broadcasting organization.

Product Information

A number of corporations are creating Web servers in the form of product catalogs. These catalogs are part of corporate customer services and prospects and customers are informed of their existence either through advertising or direct mail. In these cases, the Web helps provide answers to inquires faster than traditional help desks or human telephone response.

The catalog shopping industry includes hundreds of companies large and small, each of which would be delighted to have an interactive channel of its own. This $50 billion annual industry will have to change to sell its products through these interactive channels, otherwise it will not be able to survive a host of new and specialized home shopping firms that will take advantage of this new marketing infrastructure.

GE Plastics, a $6 billion subsidiary of General Electric, is among the first developers of an online catalog which includes 1,500 pages of product information. This catalog can be accessed by customers around the world on an around-the-clock basis. Within a month of start-up it experienced 12,000 hits. GE Plastics believes the online catalog gives them a competitive advantage because it provides answers in minutes, compared to three days using the telephone and the fastest mail deliveries.

Retail catalog companies are also developing their online versions and setting-up Web servers of their own. Specifically these include Spiegel Inc., Robert Redford's Sundance Catalog, and Land's End.

Virtual Banking Services

More than 200 banks already have established some form of Internet access or Web presence despite the lack of Internet transaction security precludes provision of full-service online banking. Many initial Web banking sites are limited to providing information about available services or online forms for credit card and loan applications.

In October 1995, the first virtual online banking service on the Web was initiated by Security First Network Bank (SFNB), a subsidiary of Cardinal Bancshares, Inc., of Atlanta. SFNB actually offers its customers full-service, 24-hour checking, and banking services. SFNB is based on a Web site using a software program called the Virtual Bank Manager, which includes a multilayered security system designed by SecureWare, Inc., a supplier of such technology to the U.S. military and intelligence services. Wachovia Corporation and Huntington Bancshares, which invested $5 million in SFNB, created a separate company called Five Paces, Inc. to license the Virtual Bank Manager software to other banks to set-up full-service banking operations on the Internet. The SFNB Web site is located at **http://www.sfnb.com.**

The SFNB home page represents a graphic image of a bank interior with several choices including information, account set-up, customer service, personal finance, security and demonstration areas. It also includes access to the bank's president, and users can use a questionnaire to provide details about themselves. Once they open an account, customers can write checks, electronically make deposits, and pay monthly bills online.

Customer Service Information

These are Web sites that actually serve customers with information both before and after they purchase company products. These are highly interactive home pages which ask the user to define product specifications, color preferences, sizes, and other parameters useful in customizing a product such as shoes, clothes or tires. The objective of these Web sites is to provide a 24-hour customer service contact that can meet most requests for information and service without requiring to maintain an expensive facility such as a help desk.

One of the best examples of a customer service Web site is that of Goodyear Tire & Rubber Company. This home page allows a user to select a specific tire for a car based on specifications and preferences. It also offers suggestions on how to prolong the tread life on the tire and provides details about the nearest Goodyear outlet. Its URL is **http://www.goodyear.com**.

Directories

Directories are lists of existing Web sites arranged in alphabetical, hierarchical or categorical order. These directories are developed and maintained by various organizations and at different sites within the Web. Those who have a home page or a Web site should register with one or more of these directories which list the specific URL address. This is an important step in making sure potential users can locate and visit a particular site.

These directories vary in size and organization. Some are very general and include numerous categories and topics, while other are more specialized and are organized by specific subject matter, business or industry. Registration and listing a home page in a directory creates a link to that home page with a number of other Web sites and resources.

Home page cross-links help increase the chances of the site being noticed and visited. For business Web sites, it is mandatory to contact a large number of directories and issue additional information about creating the presence on the Web. Web site owners are also obliged to keep track of all directories where they have listed their URL, and must inform all those sites of any changes because otherwise their home pages will become inactive links on the Web.

Yahoo (Yet Another Hierarchical Officious Oracle) is considered one of the most comprehensive directories of this type. Yahoo is often recommended as the first directory during a search because of its vast size, simplicity, clarity, and ability to access masses of other sites categorized under 18 major sectors.

Those who wish to add their Web site listing to the Yahoo directory can complete an online form accessible through the Yahoo home page itself. The form asks for the specific URL and places it in a particular category. The Yahoo directory operator verifies the listing, finds the most logical place for placement within the directory hierarchy, and notifies the Web via E-mail when the listing has been added to the directory. The URL to accomplish this is:

http://akebono.stanford.edu:8000/yahoo/bin/add

Bell Atlantic Electronic Publishing created the Interactive Yellow pages on the Web. This is another type of directory which includes 500,000 business, government, and community listings for the Washington D.C. and Baltimore areas. About 80,000 of those listings are enhanced with color and direct links to advertisers home pages on the Web. Users can search this directory by name, specific brand, product or service.

There are numerous directories where Web sites and home pages can be registered and listed and more are being created every day. Table 2.7 provides a list of representative Web directories among the most popular.

Table 2.7 Representative Directories on the Web

Web Directory	Description	URL
Bell Atlantic Electronic Publishing	Interactive Yellow Pages on the Web	http://www.yellowpages.badg.com
CERN Particle Physics Laboratory	Considered to be the mother of the Web with most extensive information	http://infor.cern.ch/hypertext/www/TheProject.html
Global Network Navigator	Among the first directories making the Internet accessible to new users	http:/www.gnn.com
Interesting Business Sites on the Web	Specialized directory maintained at Renselear Polytechnic	http://www.rpi.edu/~okeefe/business.html
Yahoo	Most extensive links of about 3,500 from other Web sites and 710,000 users per day with the keyword search facility	http://akebono.stanford.edu/yahoo

USENET Groups on Multimedia

USENET newsgroups are Web sites dedicated to specific topics. Estimates suggest there are more than 10,000 groups on the Web covering almost every conceivable topic. They provide an excellent means to obtain the latest information about various aspects of the Web including multimedia usage and content sources. USENET group sites provide FAQs which are the best indicators of the activity with a particular group. FAQs also contain rules and regulations of participation including indication of whether advertising or product announcements are permitted and with what frequency.

Individuals can create their own groups either independently or under existing USENET structures. There is a FAQ called "Creating a USENET group," which describes this complex process. It can be located at **http://www.cis.ohio-state.edu/**.

What Makes a Web Site Stand out of the Crowd

The only way to keep attracting users to a Web site and stay a winner is to keep developing the site and innovating. This is one reason why many Web sites indicate they are under "construction," but this can be dangerous if the changes are not noticeable and the users spread the word through various newsgroups.

The quality of a Web page, as seen by users, varies depending on who they are. There are a number of elements that influence how the final page will look. These include the way the page was designed and encoded with the HTML language, what browser the users will employ in reading it, and how the particular browsers are configured with regard to fonts, colors, styles, and graphics. Good Web page designers must take all those factors into consideration.

A good home page includes information about the contents of the Web site on the first 25 lines. This leaves little room for graphics or images, but icons or very small pictures can add appeal to the appearance of a Web page at the start. There is some assurance using this kind of home page information distribution the page will load relatively quickly into the user's PC and prevent frustration.

To communicate the contents quickly and effectively, good Web pages also contain text paragraphs designed with headlines with fonts that outline the contents of the page and are easy to read. In general, this means headings ranging in font sizes from 20 down to 12, which is the standard letter typing font size. It is also important to remember that browsers used for viewing Web pages take up space on the screen because they also use icons, buttons, menus and ribbons to control the screen. Thus, a well designed Web page should appear as complete as possible on most screens regardless of the browser used.

Other important characteristics of a good Web page include the latest date, author identification, feedback method, linkages, and some ranking of the importance of various elements that can be accessed from that page. Feedback availability is important because it provides a means of interacting with the users, seeking their opinions, and receiving improvement suggestions. In this instance, ready-made electronic forms with checkboxes or comment input fields are the most popular because they require minimum user effort to respond.

Chapter 3

Multimedia Strategies for the Web

A critical question to be answered when contemplating development of presence on the Web is: What is its objective? Whether multimedia or not, Internet presence in general, and Web presence in particular, can be developed and maintained for various reasons. Since there are costs associated with the development and maintenance of such presence, it makes sense to determine precisely for what purpose a Web site is being developed. This is important when a multimedia Web site is being contemplated because the costs of development – including audio, video, and animation – are considerably higher than those for a simple textual presence.

Cost is an important issue when the site involves considerable multimedia content, in the case where the Web site serves corporate marketing and public relation functions. Because access to such a Web site will be universal – available to anyone in the world – the Web site is judged continuously by many users from various countries by the content and appearance of its home page. Not the complete Web site presentation as such, but according to the appearance of the very first home page of the company. This is why it is better not to have a presence on the Web at all, rather than develop and maintain a poorly designed home page. The poor representation will reflect on the company and its products almost immediately.

The Need for Web Presence

The first issue that must be resolved by any organization is whether it needs to have a Web presence at all. It is important to remember 95% of existing Web sites in mid-1995 are considered poor by industry analysts because they are developed and maintained by computer programmers rather than professional marketing and promotion specialists. As a result, defining the objectives of a Web presence is the first step to successful Web site development and operation.

There are good reasons for not creating and maintaining a Web presence. A company whose operations are strictly local will not benefit if people from other countries learn about its activities. This type of Web presence can only be justified by public companies that want to provide financial and operational data to financial analysts and widely scattered investors, but it is questionable if the Web site is required in such cases. Mailing of quarterly reports or press releases through traditional venues will probably be more targeted and less expensive.

On the other hand, a desire to use the Web purely for promotional, institutional advertising or public relations purposes is quite legitimate. The question is whether it is worth the expense and effort to remain competitive with those willing to spend the money and time to sustain a good Web site.

When deciding whether a Web presence is needed, one must consider a number of issues including a definition of objectives, a strategy for the operating infrastructure, a decision about the basic operating system (OS), development environment considerations, and construction of the client/server (C/S) infrastructure. It is critical to discover, at the earliest possible stage, the problems and frustrations facing the developer and owner of a Web site. It is particularly important to realize there must be a commitment to updating and maintaining the Web site. If the enterprise is not prepared to budget and organize for this activity, it is better not to undertake a Web presence project unless it is clearly for research and demonstration purposes.

Once a decision to develop a Web presence has been made, however, the objective should be clearly stated to give the home page the proper direction. Table 3.1 outlines the objectives of a sample Web site.

Table 3.1 Defining Objectives of a Web Presence

Web Presence Objective	Description and Comments
Type of Audience	Internal, external or both
Simple Information Dissemination	Electronic distribution of announcements, press releases, company information
Information Dissemination with Searching Facilities	This type of presence requires design of home pages with hyperlinks to other pages of Web sites; can be added later
Interactive Inquiry and Forms Facilities for Collecting User Data	Once basic Web site includes basic information and search facilities, inquiry forms can be added, but must connect to databases
Front-end to Sophisticated Interactive Applications	This technology is being developed with the trend being to use browser tools as front-end for Web servers

Outbound Traffic Policy

A Web presence represents its sponsor and it is important to create a corporate policy that relates to the publication and deployment of Web pages and their content. Companies that fail to formulate and announce a Web policy to their departments and individual workers leave themselves open to potential problems.

The establishment of a Web presence immediately creates a need for a corporate policy that describes the Web home page's appearance and determines who within the corporation is authorized to design, develop, and maintain it. Multimedia content that will appear on the Web must be agreed upon and checked for accuracy, aesthetics, and permissions to display to the public. Because there is a potential for numerous unknown users to see the Web page, it is necessary to make absolutely sure the contents are beyond reproach with regard to cultural, racial, and religious sensitivities. Also, there is always a question as to the correct presentation of the company and ownership of the artwork, graphics or music, and video clips that may be used. In many instances, these issues are not technical. They most often concern the design, content, and authority of Web page development, rather how to make the system work.

The most important aspect of outbound Web traffic is determining who in the organization is authorized to create and locate a page on the corporate Web server. There is a considerable amount of responsibility involved and a clear authorized leader must be designated to maintain a steady and consistent Web policy. There may be a Webmaster who can handle the technicalities of Web site development and updating, but this is not necessarily always the person who will make decisions about content, appearance, and basic objectives.

Another important issue pertains to whether private and departmental pages will be allowed on the Web server, and whether a consistent design format must be followed for all pages deployed on the Web server. Some pages may be designed for access solely by internal users, but a decision also must be made whether such pages can be made available to other users outside the corporation. This question also is related to the types of restrictions that may exist on the type and quality of materials that can be published on the Web server.

Other issues that must be settled with regard to outbound Web traffic involve the question of Web addresses and its promotion in other media. The company must state clearly where, how, when, and which Web pages can be identified and advertised on the Internet or in other media to bring them to the attention of the users.

As far as implementation of an external Web server is concerned, Web page creators must have a clear understanding whether they can develop their own servers or must use a centrally available system. Associated with this question is the very critical issue of who provides and maintains the hardware and software for such a Web server.

Inbound Traffic Policy

Associated with corporate Web presence is the overall Internet activity of corporate workers who may be tempted to engage in extensive surfing binges – not only wasting corporate time and resources, but possibly exposing the company to criminal liability. Pornography, online gambling, political fringe, extremist promotions, hate speech, criminal skill, and training programs are all subject to exclusion by corporations. As a result, network managers and corporations must lay down and enforce a strict regimen of the type of outside

Web content traffic that is acceptable and have specific measures in place to deal with those who digress from the prevailing policy.

In many instances, this may require implementing special software designed to block access to certain Web sites. Network administrators may want to track user activity in specific logs to develop audit trails of Internet and Web access activity by its employees.

In some cases, blocking and logging may be combined and some of the firewalls offer facilities to implement such programs. Companies developing a Web presence must decide whether the time and effort required to monitor Internet activity is worthwhile, and if it offsets the cost associated with undesirable outbound traffic originated by its employees.

Searching Cyberspace

Prior to the development of a Web site, the existing Web home pages should be searched to obtain a feel for what type of pages work and which do not. In particular, it is important to explore competitors' Web sites because their mistakes and achievements have much to offer to new Web developers.

With the advent of new browser tools and various Web search agents, this task is becoming easier by the day. Such agents can be programmed to continuously wander the Web, looking for competitive Web sites to compare with a proposed company site.

In addition, the latest multimedia database search tools can be brought into action to exploit the Web sites for design and content ideas. Textual descriptors are not very good for searching and identifying specific multimedia materials, but new content-based search tools are now coming to market that use color, texture, shape, and position characteristics. Initial content-based query methods focused on manipulating image data because those are the most common multimedia files stored in databases and servers. Sound and video files can be searched in a similar way and there is little question that such methods are already under development.

Content-based querying of multimedia data has already attracted a number of vendors to develop specific software products to implement this technology. IBM was among the first to research this area, but the most innovative approach has been taken by Virage, Inc., of San Diego, whose principals participated in the early IBM research on this topic. The existence of these tools makes the Web a huge depository of multimedia materials and presentation ideas that can be searched efficiently by Web site designers to discover profitable ideas and content that can be reproduced.

Developing Web Pages

Ideally, there should be something new on a Web page every day to ensure visitors return to the site. At worst, industry experts suggest the Web must be updated once every six weeks. Otherwise, people will not be compelled to return.

In keeping with any commercial product, the company must try to make the Web site better as time progresses. When a decision to create a Web presence is reached, a commitment must be made to develop a maintenance and updating strategy that will keep the Web site current and interesting. When the home page is actually introduced, there must be a precise outline of how it will change and develop for at least the following year.

According to Web development and operations experts, the actual development of the home page is only 10% of the overall development effort. The remaining 90% of the effort is in updating and maintaining the site. Companies that contemplate a Web presence should keep this in mind, and plan and budget accordingly. No one should be fooled by the apparent low cost of creating a Web presence, as this may only include a monthly access fee to a third-party Web server. The real cost is in the production of a superior Web home page, and in continuously updating, upgrading, and improving the site.

Renting Web Space on a Server

Perhaps the best strategy in developing a Web presence is to start by renting Web space on a Web server maintained by an Internet access provider. This approach eliminates the need to look for Web design and development skills, and exploits the fact a Web server already exists. The immediate caveat with this approach is that all Web servers are not created equal and serious research is advisable before deciding on a particular Web server rental.

Connectivity with the Internet and the Web is accomplished directly or through Internet Services Providers (ISPs). These ISPs offer a whole range of

Internet services, many of which are extremely small and questionable services unlikely to provide a connection suitable for multimedia traffic with the Web.

The best solution is to locate a full-service ISP that is also an Internet Presence Provider (IPP). Such an organization is equipped to assist in locating and installing all necessary equipment to become a node on the Internet with a connection that has sufficient bandwidth to handle Web multimedia traffic. Use of an ISP is very popular among small- and medium-sized businesses because the setup and associated maintenance of a direct Internet connection carries a considerable cost. On the other hand, not all ISPs have the facilities and knowledge to develop a meaningful Web presence for a subscriber, which is why they must be investigated thoroughly before making a commitment.

IPPs should be able to host home pages on their Web servers and provide IP addresses and a domain name service (DNS) registration that identifies the company Web site uniquely in cyberspace, at least for the duration of its presence on the Web server of that particular ISP organization. Table 3.2 summarizes the various types of Web presence providers.

Table 3.2 Types of Web Presence Providers

Provider Category	Basic Services and Description
Limited Providers	Allow assembly of own Web pages, forms, and all necessary programming
Flexible Providers	Provide options to perform design and programming of Web pages for clients
Cybermalls	Provide single Web pages or limited design capabilities
Web Design Consultants	Assist in design of Web pages providing graphics, programming, and library science skills

Web presence providers can be classified into four major categories according to their own skills and capabilities. Some have limited skills concentrating on the operation of a Web server on which they allow clients to assemble their own Web pages. In this case, the client must possess all the Web site design skills or find assistance of yet another consulting organization.

More flexible Web presence providers have the necessary skills and may offer the option of developing Web home pages for their clients. In such cases, it is still necessary to provide the corporate resources to collaborate with the Web presence provider. Cybermalls offer even less than full-featured Web sites, often providing only a single Web page for simple announcements that may have to be developed by the actual user. Finally, there are Web design consulting forms that assist in design of Web pages and possess a full range of skills. Typical hourly fees for such work range from $50 to $100.

Advantage and Disadvantages of Web Presence Providers

There are significant advantage in using a Web presence provider rather than developing a proprietary Web server on the Internet. Web presence providers can quickly provide a presence on the Web without acquiring specialized UNIX, HTML or telecommunications skills.

On the other hand, selection of a Web presence provider is not easy and requires determination and knowledgeable research. The task of identifying Web presence providers – also known as "Web hosting sites" – is relatively simple. The problem develops when it becomes necessary to distinguish between the various Web presence provider categories to make sure the supplier of choice will meet all the corporate requirements.

By using an existing Web presence provider, the cost of a Web presence can be reduced significantly and the setup time is only limited by the amount of time it takes to gather the materials and design the home pages. However, there are a number of issues relating to bandwidth, support, server type, and pricing that must be addressed before a final decision is made.

If the Web site is to include significant multimedia content and if it is expected to generate a large number of visits, it is important to be certain that the provider can deliver sufficient bandwidth to handle the traffic. Some providers may claim T1 connectivity to the Internet, which implies 1.54 Mbps bandwidth, but the real issue is the number of other users that will be sharing that line and what provisions exist to handle peak traffic loads.

The question of Web site support is also critical because it is not under the control of the sponsor. Many Web presence providers claim 24-hour support seven days a week, but this is sometimes just answering or paging services used to locate a support specialist in an emergency. The quality of support can be readily tested by contacting a support number in the middle of the night or sending official E-mail and waiting to see how long it takes before it is answered. If the Web presence is a prototype for a 24-hour global customer service operation, the question of 24-hour support with immediate response becomes crucial.

Whether the Web presence provider sets-up the Web site on a dedicated machine or on a shared server is also important. When the Web content includes multimedia and is expected to attract large numbers of users, it will require more bandwidth than may be available on a shared server.

The other issue to consider carefully for a Web hosting service is pricing. There are no standard pricing schemes and pricing depends on various types of services. The critical issues in pricing include the minimum initial contract period, data transfer capabilities, and Web server services – all of which may carry significant incremental costs.

The data transfer capability defines the number of bits the Web server can send to Web browsers of various users. If the Web server includes multimedia content such as graphics, audio, and video, it must automatically move much more data. This is also the case when the number of users increases at the Web site and these factors often influence the price of the Web service.

Most Web presence providers allow a basic minimum number of megabytes per month of about 500 MB, beyond which additional fees accumulate automatically. There are some Web presence providers who do not have a limit on data transfer while others provide up to 2.5 gigabyte (GB) per month as part of the monthly package for $200 to $300. The data transfer issue becomes important when pricing a Web site with large amounts of multimedia content. The use of extensive graphics, animation, and video clips can deplete such monthly allowances quite rapidly.

It is also important to determine whether there are charges for making changes and updates to the Web site. Again, changes in multimedia content will generate considerable data transfer if images and prices of products are changed frequently on the home pages as they may have to be if the site is to remain competitive.

A company that anticipates heavy multimedia content on their Web site, frequent changes, and large numbers of visitors should evaluate carefully the costs of renting a Web site. Despite the high initial installation costs of proprietary Web servers, it may be more cost-effective in the long run.

Finally, whoever rents a Web site must consider the possibility of switching to another provider. It is very important to make sure initial contracts are relatively flexible and that the domain name is owned by the company. If the Web presence provider obtains the domain name for a subscriber without such provisions upfront, it may be extremely difficult to move to another provider. Yet, access providers and the nature of their services change so rapidly that it pays to remain as flexible as possible when renting a Web site.

Nevertheless, Web site renting remains a viable option because companies can provide rapid access to a Web site in an economic manner if they investigate and choose their Web presence provider wisely. They can also avoid buying expensive server hardware and software, avoid intrusion into their internal networks, and avoid creating traffic bottlenecks on their Internet links.

Table 3.3 Representative Web Presence Providers

Web Presence Provider	URL	Telephone
Cerfnet	http://www.cerf.net	619/455-3900
Cortland Electronics	http://www.cortland.com	206/217-0158
Delta Internet Services	http://www.delta.net/commerce.html	714/778-0370
Digital Express Group	http://www.digex.net/products/servers	800/969-9090
HomeCom Communications	http://www.homecom.com/services/hosting.html	404/249-9919
Internet Cafe	http://www.internet-cafe.com/icafe/services.html	805/685-0191
Maximized Online	http://maxonline.com	714/955-5300

Location of Web Sites and Servers

The physical location of Web sites and servers are irrelevant because the Internet spans the globe, thus connection and transmission charges are not based on distances between Web servers and user browsers. The location of Web servers does make a difference because it affects the distance between Internet backbone lines that carry the traffic at very high speeds. In the case of Web servers with multimedia traffic, it is necessary to use dedicated leased lines such as T1 or T3 that provide speeds up to 45 Mbps. These are primarily fiberoptic cables connecting the Web server site to the telephone company. The setup costs for these connections are very high and depend on the distance from the central telephone switch. Those who plan to set-up their Web servers must consider this fact.

Developing Web Sever Sites

A decision to develop a Web presence within the company implies availability of UNIX, HTML or other Internet telecommunications talent and creative multimedia design and marketing skills. It also implies the willingness to provide internal network security and a commitment to frequently update and maintain the Web sites.

Web server development has heavy technological connotations and companies that do not take Web server development seriously are wasting both time and money. Experienced Webmasters now suggest any Web site must be completely redesigned at least every six months, which requires corporations to have a permanent staff of experts dedicated to monitoring and upgrading the Web performance.

However, more companies are building Web servers for internal and external promotions and marketing. If this trend continues, many of the larger corporations will soon gain the required expertise to design, operate, and maintain Web servers internally or outside the secure corporate networks on the wide open Internet.

Budgeting adequately to meet the costs of staffing, hardware and software, operations, and Web content design and updating is paramount.

Hardware costs are the smallest part of the total and depend on the type of Web servers being built. An HTTP Web server can range from UNIX-based systems costing $15,000 to $50,000, through workstations in the $5,000 to $12,000 range down to a $1,500 486 PC. The most costly aspect of developing a Web server in-house is the technical expertise of the specialists required to integrate the hardware and software systems into a working whole.

While the costs are not trivial, the company with a proprietary Web server controls its contents exclusively. This is particularly important if the Web site contains multimedia documents, graphics, maps or complex diagrams and forms that require frequent attention.

To run, Web servers require multitasking operating systems such as UNIX which is now the dominant Web server system. Others in use include Windows NT, OS/2, and System 7. Web servers also require a significant amount of processing power and random access memory (RAM), both of which increase drastically depending on the type of content and number of users.

As a communications system, the Web server processor must keep up with the speed of the Internet connection to prevent bottlenecks. When a large amount of multimedia traffic is involved, a T1 link is the minimum solution – which means an installation cost ranging from $2,000 to $6,000, and $1,000 to $4,000 in monthly fees with additional mileage charges depending on distance from the central telephone switch.

Although development of Web servers in-house is clearly an expensive and continuous undertaking requiring links to databases, frequent updating, and a long-term commitment to a Web presence, companies are generally are better off developing and running their own servers. These servers should be run on dedicated computers behind firewalls to minimize the danger of external attack. A Web server not running on a dedicated system can allow hackers to gain access to corporate databases through the Internet, and companies setting-up Web presence for external operations must, therefore, take great care to assure network security.

Development of a secure Web server is a complex process that calls for a high level of specialized expertise. Any company planning to maintain a Web presence must consider this factor.

Creating Firewalls

A firewall is basically a computer installed between the internal LANs and external Internet environment designed exclusively to prohibit unauthorized outsider access through the Web site of the company. In reality, a firewall can only limit unauthorized access rather than stop it completely. Internet security experts estimate firewalls can probably stop 90% of unauthorized traffic most of the time, but it is unlikely they can constantly prevent all such traffic. This is the reality and it must be included in Web development strategies.

A firewall is a software and hardware combination that monitors, filters, and protects an internal corporate network from unauthorized access from connected external networks such as the Internet. Most firewalls are hardware-based filtering systems created at single entry point into the corporate network. Unfortunately, a single point firewall does not provide sufficient protection from unauthorized access. It is much better to implement combinations of hardware and software at several points between the initial entry point and the internal network. As a result, the best firewalls will consist of a series of components acting jointly to implement protection. Example of a firewall is shown in Figure 3.1.

Figure 3.1 A Firewall Example

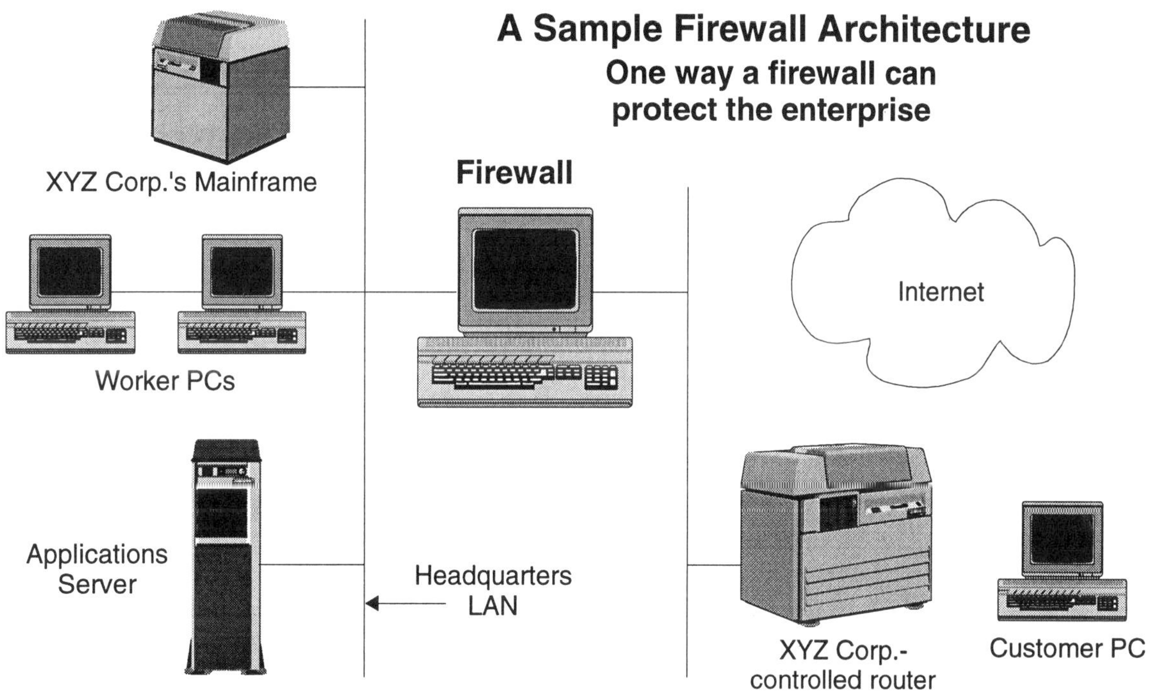

Source: Information Week

Multimedia traffic in and out of a corporate network and its Web site is very difficult to control because it combines and includes many unreliable underlying protocols. There are methods to secure individual Web protocols such as HTTP, FTP, WAIS, Archie, Gopher, and others. While such methods exist, the actual effort presents a great deal of complex work.

The problem with multipoint firewalls and multimedia transmission is the potential for latency or delays that will make real-time multimedia transmissions or video unacceptable. Firewall design in cases of Web sites that depend on real-time multimedia inputs must be carefully structured and tested to ensure the transmissions are taking place in a reasonable and acceptable manner.

The best strategies include the use of Secure HTTP (SHTTP), which provides standard hooks to plug in security features such as authentication or encryption. Another option is to use software licensing technologies for distribution and licensing of intellectual properties. Other technologies also exist which provide electronic "fingerprinting" of intellectual properties which facilitates the tracking of illegal use and distribution.

Internet firewalls that protect corporate LANs from unauthorized access by outsiders are not foolproof. Unless the firewall is designed to protect a LAN from all the potential hacker attack techniques, there is always the possibility of some unwanted outside interaction. This possibility increases as time progresses because hackers are quite capable of developing programs to keep track of all access methods tried and focus on weak links in the firewall.

This issue was originally addressed in April 1995, when the freeware program known as Security Administrator's Tool for Analyzing Networks (SATAN) was released, but it is now questioned who benefits the most from its availability. SATAN angered many network administrators because it is accessible to everyone and can assist hackers in penetrating firewalls. A need for frequent upgrading is another drawback of the SATAN software.

To solve this problem in a more business-like fashion, Internet Security Systems, Inc., developed an Internet Scanner 3.0 product that detects potential and actual loopholes in existing firewalls, Web servers, and other TCP/IP software systems. It operates by storing in memory more than 100 known hacker approaches used to gain unauthorized access. The Internet Scanner checks out specific network devices and generates a report identifying vulnerable aspects of each network while recommending appropriate solutions to make them more secure. The software includes tests for IP spoofing, firewall integrity, and Web server and E-mail security, and supports parallel scanning of numerous devices. It is available for Advanced Interactive Executive (AIX) 3.2, HP-UX, SunOS 4.x, and Solaris 2.3 operating systems and its pricing ranges from $795 for 10 devices, to $99,999 for 10,000 devices.

Firewalls must be continuously managed to ensure unauthorized access is not occurring. Unmanaged firewalls are worse than no firewalls at all and are outright dangerous, creating a feeling of complacency.

Securing against Hackers, Viruses, and Spies

Distributed enterprise networks are more vulnerable to outside attacks than centralized mainframe systems. Traditional corporate networks are based on point-to-point connections. Internet and client/server solutions introduce any-to-any connectivity which may be useful in reengineering and downsizing the corporations, but create increased risks from hackers and cyberpunks who attack backbones and corporate databases. In addition, there is a valid fear of or industrial spies who can penetrate databases with sensitive duct marketing and design information.

ecurity of corporate networks has moved from being a technical iness priority. This is particularly true when the company has or more Web sites connected to the corporate network. Each Web al gateway for external attack and all must be secured against

has three components:

;

and

to be effective, all three components must be in place and irewalls protect only the hardware.

igned to prevent access to those who are not authorized mplemented through the use of passwords, although such methods are inherently insecure. Passwords can be easily stolen, surmised or discovered using computer routines. Many end-users are also known to write down their passwords in a visible place on their computer installations. The danger always exists that, if one password is compromised, the entire network can be affected.

Authentication systems based on intelligent tokens are more reliable. These generate passwords on a one-time basis that must be verified by a secure server on the network. The best security is delivered through the use of hardware tokens similar to credit cards, but this is an expensive alternative and requires replacement of these products periodically. An easy solution are software tokens, but these are relatively easy to crack by determined hackers.

Authorization systems are means to keep users from accessing private files and records. Specifically, authorization systems deliver a secure single sign-on which permits a user to log-on once and obtain access to all applications and computers for which that user is authorized. In considering authorization schemes, it is necessary to evaluate how difficult it is to set-up, what applications it will protect, and what management capabilities are included. In global networking, another factor is freedom to export authorization software usually restricted by the government.

Encryption is also used to protect data as it is transmitted across a network, but encryption of itself does not mean authorization as such. Encryption means a mathematical algorithm that replaces one sequence of bits representing a transmission by another. Basic types of encryption in use include private and public key systems. Private key encryption is based on a secret key known to the sender and the receiver. The same key is used to encrypt and decrypt the data. The drawback is the need to find a secure way of transmitting keys between parties.

Public key encryption is based on two keys assigned to every user. A public key is freely distributed, but a private key is kept secret. In this scheme, any transmission encrypted with a public key can only be decrypted with the corresponding private key. Under this scheme, it is important to protect the private keys when they are first allocated. There are a number of vendors that supply authentication and authorization systems, some of which include encryption capabilities.

Network security also can be seen as a question of access security, payload security, and user security. Access means control of who can and who cannot use the network to and from the Web site. Payload security involves encryption, while user security is the most sensitive and difficult to implement. It involves validation of access requests for users giving them the right to read, write, modify, and manipulate data within specific or unlimited time frames.

This aspect of security is probably the most difficult to manage compared with technical security mechanisms.

The overall issue involved in transmission of multimedia content across a secure network and Web sites must be balanced against negative impact on performance of computer resources and complexity of system development and maintenance.

Requirements for 24-Hour Global Access

One of the aspects of the Web presence is the requirement to serve users on a 24-hour basis. The Web exists all around the world and there are always users who will try to access the Web site regardless of the time of night and day. This poses two problems for the Web site sponsor. One has to do with the operation of the Web server itself and the other with timely updating of the contents.

A Web site sponsor, particularly if the company plans to develop it into a commercial marketing or customer service operation, must be prepared to provide full technical support on a 24-hour basis. It is one thing to say that once the Web site is established it can run unattended. There are potential breakdown possibilities for a variety of reasons, and on occasion a site may be overloaded and the servers may not be able to handle the large numbers of simultaneous users. There is always also the possibility of hackers or competitors intentionally damaging the Web site or modifying the contents in such a way the site must be immediately taken down and restructured to correctly reflect the organization and its policies.

Updating and maintaining the site may be necessary in some cases, depending on the type of product or services being promoted. In marketing, Web sites of competitors must be continuously evaluated and immediate response may be required to protect market share or adjust product pricing. Users will sooner or later employ agents and avatars who will continuously surf the Web, evaluating competitive products and services. As a result, whoever wants to engage in this type of electronic commerce must be prepared to monitor and react to developments on the Web on a 24-hour basis. This is a cost of Web presence operation that must be considered.

Use of Web Resources

The Web itself is a great source of multimedia resources in digital form that can often be used for developing Web sites and home pages. As corporate site developers surf the Web, they should mark any Web site that contains interesting graphics, layouts or ideas in their Web browsers. Much of the material found on the Web is copyrighted, but it can be borrowed for personal use or for testing a concept. Including such materials in corporate Web presentations is another matter. Even if it cannot be used, many sites provide creative ideas that can be modified and adapted.

When selecting and downloading multimedia materials from the Web, make sure the Web browser includes all the special features and connects to the proper viewers that might be required to access and inspect many graphic, animation, and video files. The Web is a treasure trove of multimedia content, shareware, and utilities, many of which can be acquired or adapted for use on a Web site in construction.

In the Yahoo Web site, for example, there is a Computers/Multimedia area which includes a large number of demonstrations, graphics, movies, "morphs," sounds, and shareware elements. The Global Network Navigator (GNN) contains a valuable area called the Best of the Web, which is very useful in comparing and evaluating Web home pages.

There are also extensive multimedia resources on commercial online services. These services provide multimedia service forums which contain multimedia clips, shareware, and help files. There are also vendor-sponsored multimedia forums which contain huge files of company films or clips. AOL, CompuServe, and Prodigy all offer such resources and access to the Web resources.

Luring Customers to Web Pages

If it is built, will they come? This is a frequent question about Web sites, but it must be remembered this is usually the case only for well-known or well-promoted home pages.

Otherwise, a new Web home page is really unknown until someone informs several of the Web directory sites that such a new home page has been created. While there are several Web services that specialize in monitoring and listing the creation of home pages and Web sites, the burden of promotion is really on the sponsor. The company that intends to use the Web site as a promotional and marketing tool must be prepared to advertise and announce its existence using cross-linkages with other associated Web home pages, and in conventional media such as magazines, newspapers, radio, and TV. This, of course, means additional expenditures that must be carefully evaluated when justifying the development and maintenance of the Web site. In most initial phases they do not, but companies believe the Web environment is so new and unknown they cannot afford not to explore it as soon as possible.

Building Interest with Multimedia Content

There are numerous Web sites that contain multimedia content materials to be downloaded and used in the development of multimedia applications and other Web home pages. The owners of those multimedia materials often provide access and use of those materials free of charge in return for an acknowledgment of the source. In some cases, they require a link be created to the source from the Web site where these materials are being used. This is one way of gaining publicity on the Web and getting other users to visit a Web site.

Images, graphics, animation, and video clips add interest to home pages, but it is necessary to create or locate digital versions of such multimedia elements for use in a Web site. Availability of such multimedia elements in various Web servers is valuable to Web page developers.

Images and video provide an easy and accurate method of presenting company products and services and attracting more visitors to a Web site. However, users must have browsers configured to receive multimedia content to make such Web pages effective.

Some Web pages are designed specifically to provide such elements for use by third-parties. In many cases, however, Web page developers can copy existing Web elements and use them with their own text or graphics. Table 3.4 presents a list of possible sources of multimedia content for use in development of Web home pages.

Table 3.4 Web Sites with Multimedia Content Potential

Web Site	Description	URL
Free-Art	Interesting graphics for illustrating Web pages	http://www.mcs.net/~wallach/freeart/buttons.html
Internet Underground Music Archive	Free hi-fi music collection of all types of recordings	http://www.iuma.com/
Kaleidoscope	A marketplace for independent artists to sell their work online	http://kspace.com/
KNET	Rave Radio music includes sound files and JPEG movies	http://metaverse.com/knet/
MPEG Movie Archive	Numerous movies including animation, supermodels, music, space, cartoons, and music videos	http://www.eeb.ele.nl/mpeg/index.html
Photo Works	Photography exhibits and archives	http://www.bart.n.~francey/byrne.html
Rob's Multimedia Lab	Downloadable graphics, movies, and sounds of all kinds; includes links to more sound, image, and movie icons identified by icons	http://www.acm.uiuc.edu/rml/

Providing Web Search and Navigation Tools

There is a new industry emerging in relation to the Web or, rather, the Internet as a whole. It includes the development, sale, and operation of Web software tools, provision of Web access, server platforms, and system integration.

Within that group of products and services, some will be suitable for transmission of multimedia content while others efficiently handle only text and data.

Web search software in the form of agents and avatars probably presents the best opportunity for entering this market and can help identify Web sites with specific multimedia content.

Internet browsers are the major navigation tools enabling users to surf the Internet by pointing and clicking. These tools are now available in large numbers from numerous vendors in the form of freeware, shareware, and as commercial products enhanced by many computer vendors to be used with their existing products. Not all browsers can handle multimedia and the Web, but these products are improving rapidly through the addition of features to handle various video and movie viewers. The new business opportunity, if it even exists, is in development of more comprehensive multimedia browsers that can accommodate all the protocols involved in the Internet. Existing browser vendors are the companies most likely to provide such new products in this highly competitive market.

Web Servers and Access

There is a proliferation of Internet access providers throughout the world. Most are small local operations and are often resellers of Internet access. A major shakeout among Internet access providers consolidating marginal operations into larger companies, is already well under way and is expected to become more wide spread in the future.

Nevertheless, multimedia access to the Web is primarily available from the major access providers, online services, and the telecommunications companies. It is conceivable that many of the cable TV operations will become multimedia Web access providers because those companies have an existing fiber network into the households.

Whoever wants to enter this market must be prepared to compete with well-established participants. These include AT&T, BBN Planet, MCI, PSI, Sprint, and UUNET on a national basis. Regionally, companies such as Cerfbet, Netcomm, and International Discount Telecom are also significant players. Internationally, major players in Europe include Demon Internet Ltd., The Direct Connection, MAZ Internet Services, and EUnet Limited.

In terms of Web servers, this is primarily the domain of the computer hardware manufacturers – most of whom offer their top-of-the-line hardware platforms as Web servers. There seems to be a window of opportunity in this market segment for specialized servers which depend on multimedia databases pertaining to specialized subjects. For such systems to become competitive, they would have to be coupled with very efficient search agents and browsers. Yet, it is conceivable that well-matched products could present a market advantage over a random selection of hardware and software products.

Web Consulting and Development Services

Web consulting is an area that offers the greatest business opportunities, particularly to system integrators who can provide a turnkey service for design, development, and operation of client/server systems over LANs, WANs, and public services.

A major business opportunity is in the area of Internet/LAN/WAN integration, linking internal corporate networks with the Web and ensuring multimedia traffic can be efficiently handled. Integrators should be able to suggest or design client addressing schemes and user software for TCP/IP-based LANs, and provide solutions for connecting LANs that do not currently support TCP/IP protocols.

This type of integration involves considerable protocol translation concepts, network security aspects, and means to evaluate performance. System integrators involved in this consulting activity should be able to begin with bandwidth to load ratio assessments – a factor in constant flux. It is even more complex when real-time multipoint multimedia conferencing and collaborative computing come into play.

Major players in this arena are the large consulting firms and major computer hardware vendors including IBM, DEC, HP, Sun Microsystems, and others.

Conclusions

It is questionable whether it is necessary for all companies to develop a Web presence. Until it is possible to measure the results of electronic commerce in specific industries, however, most companies will invest in creating a Web site of one kind or another.

When a decision to develop a Web presence has been made, it is critical to obtain top management support and sufficient budgeting for all the aspects of Web presence planning, development, and maintenance. The existing Web cyberspace should be searched for best competitive examples of Web home pages and a clear policy of Web outbound and inbound traffic should be established before work begins.

Companies have the choice of renting a Web server or building one of their own. If the initial effort is simply to test the waters, renting a server or sharing space on an existing one is the more cost-effective way to do it. Careful screening of available Web server presence suppliers is necessary to ensure they meet access and throughput parameters, particularly where multimedia traffic is concerned.

If a company is committed to develop a Web presence for marketing reasons, it should retain control of the Web server by building its own either with in-house resources or using major consulting organizations.

Network security is a major issue in developing a Web presence and a firewall must be set-up between the outside Web site and internal corporate networks to protect it from hackers, competitors, and spies.

The Web contains numerous sites that provide multimedia content, examples, demonstrations, samples, and ideas that can be used to assist in design of a competitive home page for the company's own Web site. There are also help sites and forums from which much information and data is available about the best designs, frequency of hits in particular topic areas, and cost of operations.

The major effort in time and money that Web presence may require is the promotion of the Web site to lure customers to visit the site. This should be budgeted up front and may include cross-linking with other Web sites, and advertising and public relations efforts along traditional lines in magazines, newspapers, radio, and TV.

Development of Web presence for companies large and small is a business opportunity for providers of Web search and navigation tools, Web servers, access services, and system integrators of Web sites with existing LANs and WANs. Despite rapidly growing demands in many market sectors, the field is already overcrowded and considerable shakeout is expected in many areas.

Chapter 4

Multimedia Access to the Web

Before anything significant can be accomplished on the Web, efficient means of access must be established. If the home pages are to contain multimedia materials, they must be such that multimedia files can be retrieved without excessive delays to download extensive graphics and video materials.

Quickly and effectively powersurfing the Web requires a PC platform that is fast, has plentiful RAM capacity, uses fast modems, and is connected to the Web through an Internet access provider not only with high-bandwidth facilities, but also a reasonable number of users available on every line.

The user platform is exclusively under user control and anyone planning to engage in multimedia transmissions to and from the Web should arrange for the best available hardware and software tools at the outset. This is a basic and most important aspect of multimedia activity on the Web, and it should be optimized to provide the fastest possible platform at the user's end. The faster the processor and modem, the quicker it will access and display contents of a Web page, particularly those rich with multimedia graphics, animations, and video clips.

The user has no control over the contents of a Web page except for the one he or she develops. There is only limited control over access to the Web unless it is a server directly operated by a corporation and the users must rely on selecting the most suitable access service provider to handle multimedia traffic. Even so, the conditions within those access provider services are fluid and change constantly with varying levels of response. As a result, a very fast computer and modem combination can often compensate for slower performance at the access provider end and make the interaction less frustrating to the user.

Currently, the minimum system configuration for reasonable access to the Web is a 486/33 MHz processor with 8 MB of RAM, equipped with the appropriate graphics and video cards to handle full multimedia traffic. Slower machines will also work, but the throughput will be so poor it will be very frustrating to use. In addition, platforms without the graphics and video cards will only permit access to the textual information on a Web page and are quite useless when multimedia activity is planned.

A much better PC platform for multimedia transactions with the Web is a Pentium-based machine with speeds in the 133 MHz range or better with some of the high-performance workstations. It should have at least 8 MB of RAM, but more is recommended.

The ideal PC platform for interaction with the Web is the integrated multimedia function PC. The latest developments in the semiconductor industry suggest the appearance of a PC platform with built-in multimedia functions in a single microchip that would be integrated on the motherboard of the PC. As such, it would eliminate the need for graphics accelerators and video boards because all those functions would be included in the basic integrated circuit. These integrated multimedia PCs would also include fast modems and videoconferencing capabilities and are seen as the ultimate multimedia workstations.

The modem is a very important component of the Web access arrangement. Modem prices have dropped significantly while simultaneously providing dramatic performance increases. For multimedia Web traffic, a 28.8 Kbps modem is absolutely necessary and well worth the extra investment. Web sites will display twice as fast with a 28.8 Kbps modem than with the more common 14.4 Kbps. This becomes very important when numerous Web sites are visited and it makes a significant difference in the time spent online. If access provider charges by the hour, a fast modem is less expensive in the long run.

Perhaps the most critical aspect of multimedia access to the Web is the selection of the local access provider. This aspect of Web access is outside of user control and the selection must be made very carefully to ensure the access provider's connectivity with the Internet is adequate to provide reasonable multimedia transmissions, and that the loading per telephone line is not such that it results in busy signals and slow throughput. To surf the Web, not all connections are sufficient and a minimum of a serial line interface protocol (SLIP) connection is required.

Establishing Access to the Web

There are thousands of ISPs that offer local, regional, national, and international access to the Web. Anyone contemplating Web sites with multimedia content is limited to ISPs that can provide high-speed bandwidth connectivity in an area of interest to the Web presence developer. ISPs offering inexpensive SLIP or Point-to-Point Protocol (PPP) linkages do not have Web multimedia connectivity and cannot be taken into consideration for this purpose.

The selection of an ISP with existing high-speed connections must also be made very carefully. It is necessary to determine how many points-of-presence (POPs) the ISA offers that are capable of providing reasonable multimedia connectivity. Another important aspect to be investigated is the number of clients on ISA Web servers and the potential for communications bottlenecks and delays deadly to multimedia transmissions.

Pricing structures for Web access – particularly when high-speed multimedia-capable links are involved – vary widely from one ISP to another. Given two or more ISPs with acceptable services, a detailed price comparison must be made to discover the best possible combination of pricing options.

Because the Internet and the Web are growing rapidly, the entire service environment is in constant flux, with competitive offers announced on a daily basis. Any decision to subscribe to a particular service must consider this and any contracts signed should be either short-term or flexible enough to allow the company to change ISP and take its assigned URLs to the new location. All such arrangements must be made in advance to avoid problems of URL ownership and transfer at a later date.

Multimedia Access Bandwidth Requirements

Multimedia transmissions to and from a Web site depend first and foremost on the bandwidth of the transmission facility. Bandwidth is a measure of the amount of data that can be transmitted over a particular link in a specific unit of time. It is important to remember the bandwidth of the connection to the Web is not uniform and the slowest link will govern the overall transmission speed. It is imperative in the case of transmitting multimedia content that all the component transmission links are as fast as possible.

In the case of common data modems, bandwidth can range from 300 bits per second (bps) to 28.8 kilobits per second (kbps). Only the highest modem speeds will be adequate to provide acceptable Web multimedia connectivity. The popular Ethernet LAN bandwidth is 10 Mbps – which is more than adequate for transmission of multimedia traffic. In most cases, however, it must be shared with a large numbers of users, which means 10 Mbps is not necessarily available to a particular end-user at any time.

LANs and WANs are now generally overloaded by interactive traffic of all types and companies are upgrading the capacities of these networks to 100 Mbps. There are several alternatives to provide higher speed bandwidth capacity including switched Ethernet, Fast Ethernet, Fiber Distributed Data Interface (FDDI), Copper Distributed Data Interface (CDDI), isochronous Ethernet, Fibre Channel, and Asynchronous Transfer Mode (ATM). Segmented and switched Ethernet LANs can provide up to 10 Mbps bandwidth per user, while ATM networks can run up to 155 Mbps with the capability of providing up to 25 Mbps to the desktop. This approaches the estimated limit of 27 Mbps to a single user which can handle up to eight, real-time, multiuser, multimedia transmissions and is considered the ultimate bandwidth required by a single corporate user.

The problem with Web pages is that they contain an unexpected amount of multimedia content, and therefore, it is impossible to plan for all Web pages to efficiently download. On one hand, the Web page may consist of a number of multimedia objects of different sizes and varying compression ratios transmitted by users with different bandwidth capabilities. The safest solution is to plan for the most demanding content – full-motion video – and the use of a link that can handle such content in a reasonable amount of time at an acceptable cost. This issue becomes critical with Web page developers who must be able to communicate with the Web site in an efficient manner to develop and test the Web pages on the servers. Table 4.1 illustrates some typical multimedia objects, their size, and bandwidth requirements after compression.

Table 4.1 Typical Bandwidth Requirements for Multimedia Objects

Multimedia Content	Average Size	Compression Ratio	Required Bandwidth
A page of text	5 KB	Data 4:1	1.3 Kbps
24-bit image	7 MB	JPEG 100:1	74 Kbps
Voice and audio	64 Kbps	Audio 8:1	8 Kbps
Stereo audio	88.2 Kbps	MPEG 8:1	12 Kbps
Full motion video	45 Mbps	MPEG 50:1	1 Mbps

Network bandwidth is clearly the determining factor in multimedia Web performance. Voice, graphics, audio, and video require a significant amount of storage and bandwidth to transmit in a reasonable time. One minute of a full-screen uncompressed video without the sound requires about 300 MB. The required bandwidth is significantly reduced with compression, but if the application calls for real-time, full-screen videoconferencing, the end-user must be equipped with sufficient bandwidth to participate.

With real-time delivery of multimedia transmissions, latency and jitter are issues to be considered. These are effects that a stream of multimedia data experiences as it travels from a Web source to its destination through a number of switches, hubs, and routers while being switched through various networks. Real-time multimedia presentations must be delivered in a continuous stream because delays are unacceptable. This is only possible with high-speed networks and reliable hardware and software components to ensure continuity.

The most common multimedia Web transmissions take place in the "store and forward" mode. Multimedia files reside on a Web server and users with appropriate client software can retrieve and view those files at their convenience, but not in realtime. This method of delivery is not bandwidth-dependent, and multimedia files can be delivered over a narrow bandwidth link as long as the user patiently waits for the content to download. Depending on the slowest user link, such downloading of multimedia content may take minutes or even hours depending on the complexity of the Web home pages.

Types of Connections

There are various ways of connecting with the Internet and the Web, some of which do not provide access to the multimedia content of the Web and only result in textual information. For use of the Web with multimedia content, it is necessary to select certain forms of connectivity – a specific type of account from an Internet access provider.

Companies can access the Internet in several ways, depending on their objectives. If the purpose is to use Web for doing business, access may have to be developed through a firewall and leased lines with high-bandwidth capacity. In all cases, companies will need to connect to an Internet access provider capable of transmitting multimedia traffic at an acceptable rate to all the areas of interest to the company. Figure 4.1 illustrates alternative ways to connect to Internet access providers.

Figure 4.1 Methods of Accessing the Internet

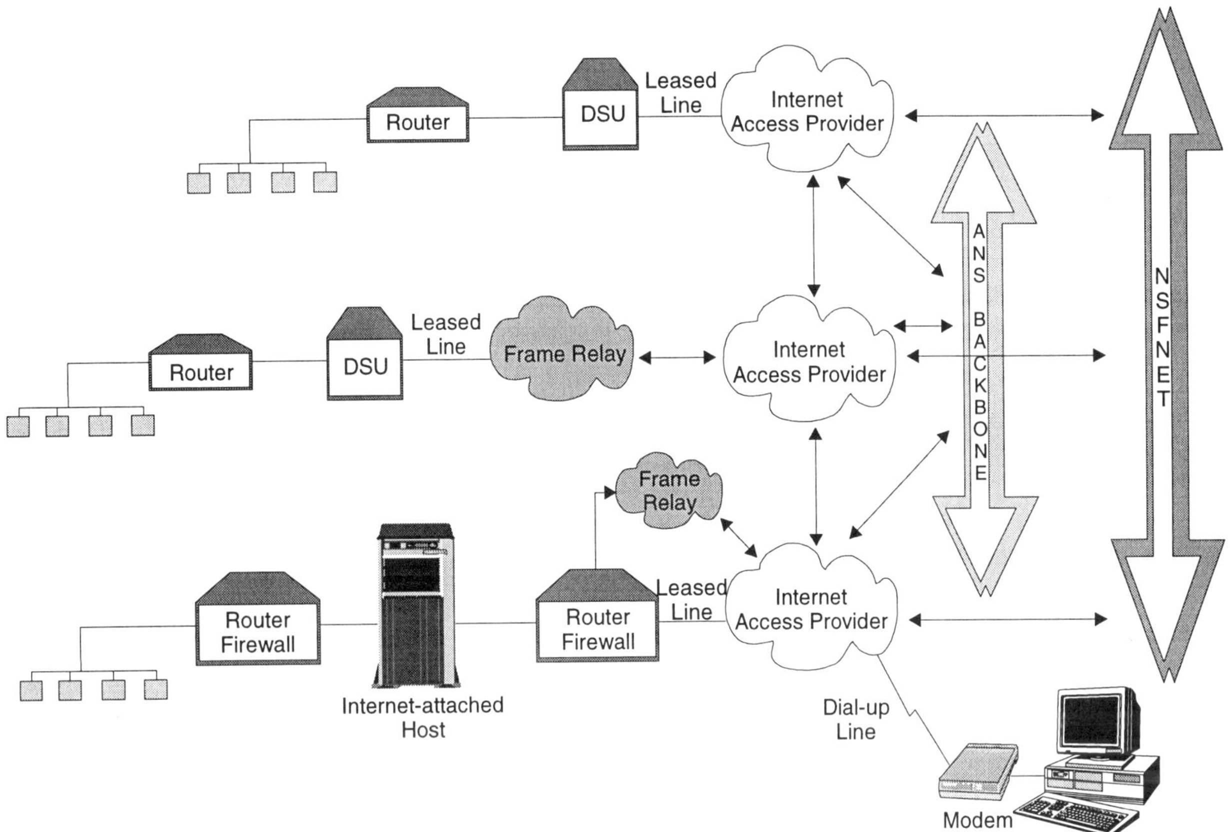

The shell accounts of an Internet access provider allow the user to log-on to a UNIX computer on the Internet, but are not suitable for using the graphical interfaces and retrieve the multimedia contents of the Web. To view multimedia Web pages, the user computer must be connected directly to the Web through a SLIP or PPP account using the fastest available modems.

There is a fundamental difference between a connectivity account for a person as opposed to a computer. When a user connects with a UNIX computer, the user is using a remote computer linked to the Internet. With a SLIP or PPP account, the Internet is extended to the PC of the user. Because the graphical interfaces such as Web browsers are designed to directly use the Internet it is necessary to be on the Internet to take advantage of those tools. To directly connect the user PC to the Internet, it is necessary to bring the TCP/IP protocol of the Internet to the PC. This is accomplished using the SLIP or the PPP accounts.

The actual connections can be made through telephone lines and modems to an Internet access provider, but many large businesses purchase a faster connection facility than that available through modems and telephone lines. These may include direct leased lines, Integrated Services Digital Network (ISDN) or Frame Relay services, which provide higher transmission speeds. Table 4.2 summarizes the different types of possible connections and the corresponding available bandwidths as Internet access alternatives.

Table 4.2 Types and Speeds of Internet Connections

Type of Connection	Bandwidth Capacity
Dial-up shell access	0.3 Kbps to 28.8 Kbps
Dial-up SLIP/PPP access	9.6 Kbps to 28.8 Kbps+ Faster modems of 38.4 Kbps and 56.8 Kbps exist but many lines are not sufficient to take advantage of those; minimum connection for downloading Web content is 14.4 Kbps
Switched 56 leased lines	56 Kbps single channel service not available everywhere; best for data transmission and initial Web interaction at moderate cost
ISDN services	Basic rate 56 Kbps to 144 Kbps; primary rate up to 1.54 Mbps; not universally available
Fractional T-1	256 Kbps to 1.28 Mbps is best option for small networks that expect to grow around a Web site or server
Leased lines	T-1 up to 1.544 Mbps is the basic standard for graphics and Web surfing available as switched or dedicated service; T-2 6.312 Mbps seldom used in practice; T-3 45 Mbps used in backbones and carrier services; T-4 273 Mbps used in carrier services
Cable TV networks	4 Mbps to 10 Mbps with interactive TV services
Frame Relay	A range of speeds fro 56 Kbps to 1.544 Mbps; not suitable for multimedia traffic but seen as intermediate form in migrating to ATM
SMDS	1.544 Mbps access – 45 Mbps operation used by Internet service providers; good for time insensitive multimedia traffic; designed as a step toward ATM
ATM	25 Mbps, 45 Mbps, 155 Mbps, 622 Mbps up to 2.5 Gbps; suitable for interactive multimedia, videoconferencing, collaborative work; expensive; used for backbones but eventually seen as only scalable technology suitable for connection-oriented transfer of video at any desirable data rate with very low latency and no interblock jitter

It is important to keep in mind there are thousands of ISP, each offering several forms of access to the Web. The major issue for the manager responsible for developing such access is to evaluate and select those that will best adhere to the individual requirements to accommodate multimedia traffic.

Serial Line Interface Protocol

SLIP was the first to provide direct Internet connectivity using standard, dial-up telephone lines. This became practical in recent years through the use of high-speed modems. When the 14.4 Kbps modems came to market, it became possible to connect PCs to the Internet. At the same time, SLIP software made it possible to extend the TCP/IP protocol from the central networks to the PC users in offices and at home. SLIP was not a planned solution and for several years was not standardized or reliable. Nevertheless, it worked, and by default became the early standard for connecting to the Internet through a telephone line.

SLIP is the minimum protocol that will provide access to Web multimedia content and, although it is practical with 14.4 Kbps, faster modems such as 28.8 Kbps and higher are recommended for use with multimedia traffic on the Web.

Point-to-Point Protocol

The PPP was originally developed for handling communications between routers in corporate networks. It is now found in devices used to communicate via ISDN and is often used instead of SLIP protocol because it is faster.

PPP can carry many protocols in addition to basic TCP/IP over a variety of connections. It can be used to link Novell or Macintosh networks while carrying TCP/IP for an Internet connection. As a result, PPP works over a corporate LAN or on computers linked directly to each other and is clearly the more robust and flexible of the access protocols.

To establish a PPP connection with a particular OS of the multimedia platform, it is necessary to use two software elements. One is a TCP/IP driver and the other is the PPP software, which controls the modem and makes the connection to the Internet service provider. In the case of Windows 3.1, Windows for Workgroups or Macintosh, special PPP software packages are required. In the case of Windows 95, Windows NT or OS/2 Warp, all is included in the OS.

Internet Services Providers

ISPs buy relatively high-speed communications line from a telecommunications carrier and splits it into channels that are, in turn, resold to local business and individual users. Table 4.3 is a summary of major ISPs providing Internet access with sufficient bandwidth alternatives to handle Web multimedia traffic.

Table 4.3 Summary of Major Internet Services Providers

Internet Service Provider	Basic Services	Telephone/Contact
ANS	80 POPs in U.S.	914/789-5300
AT&T	580 POPs in U.S.	http://www.att.com
AT&T Asia Pacific	Hong Kong base covers Asia, Pacific, and U.S.	852/2511-5828
BBN Planet	72 POPs in U.S.	617/873-3300
CompuServe	380 POPs in U.S., 73 internationally	614/457-8600
EUnet Communications	Based in Europe, U.S., and Netherlands	31 20 623-3803
GES	15 POPs in U.S., one in Mexico	609/897-7300
IBM Global Network	350 POPs in U.S., 100 POPs internationally	914/641-5000 33-1-41-88-66-00 (Paris)
Infonet	International	310/335-2600
I Star Internet	Canadian cities	613/780-2200
MCI International	400 POPs in U.S.	770/668-6000
Netcom Online	190 POPs in U.S.	415/983-5950
Pacific Bell	California region	415/542-1162
PSI	225 POPs in U.S., U.K., Japan	703/709-0300
Pipex	Europe and U.S.	44-1223-250-100
Sprint	320 POPs in U.S.	913/624-3000
Sprint International	Europe and U.S.	703/689-6000
Transpac SA	Europe based in France	33-1-45-38-88-67
US West	Midwestern region	303/965-9286
Uunet Technologies	100 POPs in U.S., 20 internationally	703/204-8000

Most ISPs offer dedicated access ranging from 56 Kbps up to 45 Mbps and dial-up access or ISDN access, but the choice of these alternatives varies from one ISP to another. A large majority operate their own servers and facilities to host customer Web pages or sites. Some companies operate national backbones and a few already claim international capabilities. Several regional access providers also operate their own backbones including routers and servers and transmission facilities. All of them are linked through the six official network access points (NAPs) in the United States which are the Internet locations where all ISPs must converge exchanging traffic on a continuous basis.

A complete list of ISPs can be found on the Web at:

http://www.primus.com/providers/

The challenge is to locate an ISP and acquire sufficient information to determine whether the service will meet all the multimedia traffic requirements. It is important to determine who in the enterprise requires access to the Web, the objective, and the global points of contact necessary to accomplish the goal. Once these issues are settled, it is possible to locate and evaluate ISPs based on specific capabilities such as bandwidth, coverage, congestion, security, servers, redundancy, access, and set-up and operation costs. Table 4.4 summarizes the major issues that should be considered when researching alternative ISPs.

Table 4.4 Internet Access Provider Checklist

Major Issue	Points to Check
Points of Presence	Number of POPs indicates coverage and Internet interconnections on a national or regional basis
Access Options	Represents possible choice o various bandwidth dedicated lines, dial-ups, and ISDN options
Backbone Topology	Evaluate bandwidth available between POPs, backbone, NAPs, and redundancy
Subscriber Ratios	Usage patterns between busy Web servers and backbone segments
Web Servers	Availability of own Web server or shared server and options to change from one to the other
Web Hosting	What Web hosting services are available, at what cost, and how many users are already online
Utilization Reports	Can electronic commerce be handled by the ISP, are utilization reports available, and are these standard or available at additional cost
Security	What levels of security are available and at what cost? Are firewalls and encryption products in the basic service package?
Pricing Structures	Prices vary depending on access type, installation costs, monthly fees, and may or may not include customer premises equipment

Determining the Coverage of a Provider

The ISP infrastructure is the first issue to be evaluated. An ISP being considered as a vehicle for developing, maintaining, and accessing a corporate Web site, server or home pages with multimedia traffic should possess significant resources and coverage. As a starting point, the ISP should be able to provide a complete map of its backbone and POPs. This is important because multimedia Web developers and users must obtain a dedicated line to the POP of their chosen ISP. As a result, the ISP with POPs nearest to the offices of the corporation will also be the least expensive to install and operate. On the other hand, many ISPs are prepared to establish a new POP in a location where none exist if a customer can be found who is willing to commit to a T-1 line or better in that location. Dedicated access to the nearest POP is a negotiable issue and this aspect should not be overlooked.

Network managers should also keep in mind that not all POPs are directly connected to the ISP backbone. A leased line to what appears to be the nearest POP may actually link the user with another POP of the ISP in another location. This process may occur before it connects with a backbone which introduces the potential for latencies and delays that will affect multimedia transmissions to and from the Web.

What Access Options Are Available?

Most ISPs provide several access options including dedicated lines, dial-up access, and ISDN access. However, not all services provide all the options or incremental bandwidth capacities within each option.

The range of dedicated access line bandwidth varies from one ISP to another. The most common is dedicated access ranging from 56 Kbps to 1.544 Mbps, but a few offer a wider range starting at 19.2 Kbps. Dedicated lines are preferred by corporate users who plan to operate Web sites or servers with multimedia content because dedicated services are also easy to integrate with corporate LANs.

For multimedia video, a 56 Kbps line transmits a jerky image of eight to 15 frames per second (fps) on a partial screen so it has limited value if real-time video is to be transmitted for promotional purposes. For full-motion, full-screen video and audio, a T-1 connection with 1.544 Mbps bandwidth is barely adequate. Yet most ISPs offer such links, thus their cost depends on the distance between the company office and POPs of the service provider and must be carefully evaluated.

It is also important to determine whether fractional T-3 links can be obtained when the T-1 capacity is outgrown by a company. This may happen quite quickly with numerous users accessing multimedia content on Web sites. Some providers including GES, Performance Systems International (PSI), and UUNet are offering a range of high-speed links from 3 Mbps to 45 Mbps in increments of 3 Mbps or other multiples. Because T-3 links are expensive fractional T-3 availability may turn out to be very cost-effective.

Dial-up access is being developed by all ISPs although not all providers currently offer it. Even 28.8 Kbps bandwidth is not suitable for efficient multimedia traffic on the Web. In cases where users can tolerate lengthy periods for downloading multimedia content from Web sites, the availability of dial-up access of this type is important as the low-cost alternative.

Slower dedicated lines may be adequate for some remote users, but ISDN links are considerably better and often less expensive. Only a few ISPs offer this type of connections although many providers claim future availability. Users interested in ISDN access should request data on availability and time frames for installation in writing when considering such alternatives.

Scrutinizing the Backbones

One of the most important aspects of an ISP is the backbone bandwidth and topology it uses to transmit data across the Web. A map of the ISP network indicates the backbone bandwidth, redundancy, and interconnections with the NAPs. Figure 4.2 illustrates such a backbone map for ANS.

Figure 4.2 Typical Internet Access Network Topology Map

ANS designs, develops, and operates high performance wide area data networks for business, research, education, and Government organizations. It operates a nationwide 45 Mbps TCP/IP public data network and provides Internet connectivity. The ANS backbone is composed of leased digitial transmission lines capable of carrying data at T3 (45Mbps) speed. The circuits are connected in a mesh topology with packet switches, or routers, located where transmission circuits intersect. Cities at these intersection points indicate core network (entrance) nodes.

Any ISP with a backbone bandwidth of less than T-3 or 45 Mbps should be considered inadequate for effective Web multimedia traffic. Many providers use a combination of T-1 and T-3 circuits in their backbones with routers and switches not conducive to the most efficient multimedia traffic transmissions.

The overall map of an ISP should be examined in relation to existing usage patterns. These are indicated by the existence of Web servers most frequently accessed and compared with the bandwidth linking them to the backbone. Many providers claim to operate T-3 backbones, but in many instances, high-frequency servers may be linked with T-1 and fractional T-1 links and such lower speed connections could present potential traffic bottlenecks. In many cases, the slowest link will dictate the overall transmission speed despite faster links available on other sectors of the backbone.

Regional ISPs may also offer T-1 access to their networks which may operate on T-1 backbone throughout the area. However, if their link to the nearest NAP is slower, it will create a major bottleneck when multimedia traffic is transmitted outside of the region.

One common practice of ISPs is the sale of numerous T-1 access lines to their network, which is also connected to the nearest NAP with another T-1 line. When several companies attempt to operate simultaneously, traffic will become congested. ISPs should be questioned about their user-to-line ratio in such circumstances, and when more than four T-1 access lines connect to a single T-1 NAP, there should be provisions for introduction of additional capacity.

ISPs sometimes announce "T-3-capable" facilities where none exist. This is possible because even the lowest 14.4 Kbps connection can be replaced by a T-3 link to make it T-3 capable. Such claims must be confirmed on the map showing actual bandwidths of existing circuits.

Redundancy is another relevant issue. Well-engineered backbones should offer alternative paths of additional bandwidth. Each existing path in a service should be backed-up by an alternate route of equal bandwidth to assure continuity if a circuit fails or there is a network outage. The shortest and most direct connection between an ISP POP and the Internet is not necessarily the safest and fastest unless there are alternative routes available in case of transmission link malfunction.

Many low-cost ISPs connect to the Internet through a single NAP. This is also a danger sign. If the particular line or equipment on it goes down, all customers of that ISP lose connectivity to the Web.

The various ISPs along the paths also must have transmission agreements with each other. In the absence of such arrangements, ISPs often include filters in their routers that deny access to traffic from ISPs with which no such agreements exist. Adequate peering arrangements are critical to smooth operation of an ISP and its ability to exchange traffic freely with other ISPs. Theoretically, a well-engineered network can succeed with just two peering locations where different ISPs come together to exchange traffic. To be safe, it is better to choose an ISP that has several peering locations providing additional redundancy or operations.

Web Server Questions

Web presence developers face an immediate choice of developing the Web pages on company-owned and operated Web servers or storing it on a Web server operated by the ISP. Operation of a Web server is a considerable responsibility and when all the costs are evaluated, it is five to six times more expensive than renting space on an ISP Web server.

ISP Web servers are typically shared by various customers, which is why their costs are relatively lower. It is important to determine whether the service provider operates a single server or manages "farms" of servers linked with LANs or FDDI backbones, which in turn, connect with the Internet. Depending on the corporate requirements, it is possible to lease an entire server from the ISP. Monthly fees vary according to server capacity, security, and bandwidth of connecting links.

Whether it is worth leasing a shared or dedicated Web server from an ISP depends on traffic congestion. Some service providers monitor the amount of traffic on a Web server and inform customers when they should move to a dedicated server. When there are more than 5,000 hits per minute, it is time to move. Make sure the ISP service provides such capability.

When a company is using a shared Web server, ascertain which other ISP customers are also located on the same server. Some users, depending on the nature of their business, may run promotions that could monopolize the server for long periods of time, creating bottlenecks and delays. This problem is alleviated by some ISPs that shift the load to other Web servers when congested.

Congestion also will become a problem if the ISP of choice does not offer enough bandwidth to the Internet NAPs. Most Web servers use T-3 45 Mbps backbones for this purpose, but some organizations such as MCI and UUNet have dual T-3 links in operation as a contingency for handling traffic overloads. ISPs that use T-1 or slower links for connecting Web server should be avoided because multiple servers require higher bandwidth. The recommended procedure is to determine the bandwidth of the backbone links and test a number of Web sites for locating one with the least congestion over a representative period of time. The user should have the freedom to move to a better Web server site when conditions warrant.

Some ISPs also provide duplicate Web servers in staging areas where clients can update their home pages while original content is accessible to Internet users. Not all ISPs provide such staging areas. Changes and updates must be made during off-peak periods or at night. This may not be practical if a Web server is involved in international commerce and must be operational on a 24-hour basis.

Checking for Web Hosting Services

Companies contemplating use of the Web as an online marketing tool must develop a competitive Web site representing their company. This requires the development of home pages in-house, putting them on the Web server operated by an ISP, hiring a specialist in Web page development or using an ISP that provides such a service.

A majority of ISPs operate their own servers and host customer pages, but the extent of this expertise differs widely. Many ISPs that look as attractive providers because of their low prices, may only operate as an access service without sufficient skills or resources to host client home pages or a Web server.

Major national and regional ISPs who offer shared or dedicated Web servers to clients also provide home page development services either in-house or through subcontractors. It is important to determine how Web hosting services are priced and the quality of their productions. ISPs have several alternative pricing schemes including startup fees, monthly fees, usage fees, and storage fees based on server space requirements.

It is possible to determine which customers currently on Web servers have used ISP development services, and the ISP should have the statistics to back-up the popularity of particular pages. Some ISPs will accept request for proposals (RFPs) for home page development, while others offer home page templates to which consumers can add images and graphics. The problem with templates is that all home pages start to resemble one another and it is hard to differentiate one company Web site from another except through unusual graphics or multimedia content. The question then arises whether the templates are suitable to include such multimedia content and whether sufficient talent exists at the ISP to performs such services.

Available Utilization Reporting

Use of a Web site on the Internet without the ability to track generated traffic is not practical for marketing applications. As a result, most ISPs prepare some form of usage reporting, detailing the number of hits and identifying the domain names of users who access a particular home page.

It is important to ascertain what utilization reports are available as part of the basic access and Web hosting service, and if additional reports can be obtained at an extra cost. In the case of BBN Planet, for example, the provider can prepare detailed reports listing according to country of the users who access the Web site at an additional charge. More importantly for Web pages with multimedia content, detailed reports can be prepared showing which pages were transmitted and the time of their transmission.

This type of reporting is crucial for evaluating the most popular content and products on a Web site, but it is not necessarily available from all ISPs. Other ISPs offer utilization reports at various levels of detail, some free of charge and others at additional monthly fees.

The Web presence operator should also consider the availability of third-party reporting software for keeping track of Web traffic. This may be more appropriate given the objective. The issue in this case revolves around the question of permission to use such a feature on a Web server of an ISP, particularly when the provider offers reports for an additional fee. These issues must be resolved by the user before signing on with a particular service.

What Security Facilities Are Needed?

Once a corporate gateway to the Web is established, security measures are required to control the traffic to and from internal networks. All ISPs offer basic security to its customers, which begins with packet filtering on their routers.

The most common security feature among ISPs is the firewall which is usually developed by third-party companies and is resold by ISPs to their customers. These firewalls can be configured in many ways, beginning with user log-on and passwords procedures to control of certain user access to specific Web servers during specific times on particular days. ANS developed its own proprietary firewall known as the Interlock. It is available to customers at a price of $42,400, including maintenance for the first year or it can be leased for $19,000 annually.

Firewalls offer a measure of protection against unauthorized access through Web sites into corporate networks. However, when companies share a Web server or rent one from an ISP, they depend on security provided by the service. Firewalls must provide security but also must handle multimedia traffic that may grow to be quite massive during peak transmission periods.

When multimedia transmissions are involved, firewalls are seen as another barrier introducing latencies and delays. Most firewalls can handle moderate traffic loads from T-1 connections, but they vary in performance and often require changes in applications to operate. Web presence developers must consider all these factors when evaluating various ISP alternatives.

In some cases, a company may operate a secure Web server while the ISP provides all administration and billing for access and business transactions. Some ISPs such as MCI are willing to work with a corporate client to develop a customized, secure Web site.

ISPs offer mostly firewalls but some also provide secure routers and encryption equipment. In addition, MCI is planning to provide SHTTP for its software which encrypts all data from a session. These are security elements vital to the development of electronic commerce on the Web, but ISPs are only just beginning to provide such features.

Most secure transaction services on ISPs are in development and standards are still not finalized. These transactions require a credit card authorization system, but most ISPs do not have a link to the banking industry to implement this feature. Nevertheless, Web presence builders should investigate ISP plans to provide such services in the future if they intend to engage in electronic commerce on the Web.

Pricing Structures of ISPs

The cost of Web access and presence depends on a number of variables including type and speed of leased lines, customer premises equipment, rental of the Web server or space, development of Web pages, files storage and maintenance, startup fees, monthly charges, and utilization reporting requirements.

The cost of the simplest dial-up access to the Web is in form of startup fees, monthly charges for a specific number of hours, and extra charges for additional hours over the limit. These changes vary from $15 startup fees, $20 monthly charge for 90 hours, and $0.75 for additional hours with I Star; to $300 monthly charge and $1.50 to $5.00 per hour for corporate dial-up accounts with CompuServe. In these cases, it pays to use the fastest available modems to shorten transmission time.

ISDN access charges a one-time fee, and assesses time charges by the minute or the hour. These charges range from $35 for 35 hours and $1.50 for additional charges with GES, to $495 startup and $495 monthly charge for unlimited usage offered by UUNet. For multimedia transmissions and basic videoconferencing, ISDN is the minimum access required to provide an acceptable quality service of this type. Many of the major national and regional ISPs do not yet offer the ISDN alternative and users considering that option should check the availability of ISDN services in the locations where the most traffic is likely to occur.

Leased-line access is the most expensive and includes installation charges and monthly fees, which may depend on a requirement to sign a minimum one-year contract. Some IPSs also offer usage-based charges and there are many levels of services available ranging from access line leasing to turnkey operations.

The typical monthly fee for a basic 56 Kbps access is about $1,000 and usually includes a router and customer premises equipment but the local access line is not included. ISPs can order and manage a local line for their clients, but there will be an installation charge ranging from $300 to $5,000, depending on distance between the corporate office and POPs of the ISP.

Typical monthly fees for T-1 1.544 Mbps access is considerably more expensive, ranging from $2,500 to $3,000. There are also installation charges for the dedicated T-1 lines which can range in cost from $300 to more than $5,000, depending on distance covered. T-1 line is now the most common option as corporations outgrow smaller capacity connections with increasing use of the Web.

ISPs do not publish prices for T-3 45 Mbps access to their networks, but these are significantly higher and ranges from $12,000 per month at PSI to $49,000 at UUNet. Since there is a very great jump between T-1 and T-3 access, some

ISPs are offering fractional T-3 access ranging from 3 Mbps to 45 Mbps. Speeds of 4, 10, 16, and 34 Mbps are available from some providers. PSI offers a 10 Mbps service for $4,000 per month.

Prices vary so much that companies should consider getting bids from several competing ISPs to determine which provides the best and most cost-effective solution. The situation in the ISP business is very fluid and competition is such that users may find more cost-effective services after they have signed-up with another ISP. It is, therefore, important to negotiate the terms of these contracts to include sufficient flexibility to move to another ISP when better terms are available. In this connection, however, the user must make sure the company owns the URL and are is to move that address to another ISP.

Web Access through Online Services

Although most major online services now offer access to the Internet and the Web, they do not generally provide full range of services available in cyberspace. The Web, in fact, represents a significant threat to online services.

According to Forrester Research, Inc., the value of the online market was estimated at $900 million in 1995, and it will more than triple to over $3 billion by 1998. On the other hand, the online service industry is concerned the number of users connecting with the Internet's Web is growing much faster than customers of proprietary online services, making the future revenues of these services questionable.

Forrester Research expects a decline of online service user population beginning about 1997, when users of online services and the Web will each be about 10 million people. According to this prediction, Web users will connect with the Internet at an accelerated pace, which will become more secure and attractive as time progresses and will offer many interactive multimedia features. Simultaneously, online service subscribers will start declining to about 7 million users by the year 2000. At that time, Web users are expected to reach more than 22 million people and the combined total of online users will be close to 30 million people. This growth is illustrated in Table 4.5.

Table 4.5 World Wide Web and Online Services

	1995	1997	2000
Online Service	7,000,000	10,000,000	7,000,000
WWW	3,000,000	10,000,000	22,000,000

Source: Forrester Research

Consequently, online services are rushing to provide Web access, but they have a major problem in this regard. Online services provide relatively low-speed access – primarily dial-up 14.4 Kbps modems, although most are upgrading to 28.8 Kbps speeds. Nevertheless, ISDN and other high-speed connections necessary for multimedia Web interaction and electronic commerce are not generally available. Corporations and merchants can join one or more cybermalls operated by the online services, but there is little opportunity to develop and operate an independent Web site as can be obtained from ISPs.

A major drawback of online services is that they are primarily set-up as information distribution and retrieval systems based on large mainframe computers. As a result, it is difficult and expensive to establish a Web presence through an online service. Online services are not set-up to host Web pages and, although it can be done, it is not a standard transaction. CompuServe provides ISP services with some high-speed access to the Internet and corporate accounts, and AOL owns ANS, a major ISP service in its own right. Microsoft Network and Prodigy are the other two online services that provide access to the Web similar to that of their competitors.

The online services established some years ago as interactive value-added networks based on text and graphics are now finding themselves competing with all the other interactive multimedia services. These services are developing new multimedia user interfaces (MUI) and some have acquired multimedia marketing and content development ventures to enhance their ability to compete in this new environment.

Most of the leading online services have already established Web servers and provide access to Internet for their subscribers. The major online services are also testing ISDN access in some areas, although, on the whole, ISDN is generally not available through these services. Table 4.6 summarizes the Web access capabilities of major online services.

Table 4.6 Web Access of Major Online Services

Online Service	Web Access Characteristics
America Online	♦ POPs in 600 cities in the United States ♦ Provides some 28.8 Kbps speed lines ♦ ISDN access is being tested in selected areas ♦ Provides a Web browser ♦ Owns ASN ISP organization ♦ $9.95 per month for five hours, $2.95 per additional hour
CompuServe	♦ POPs in 420 cities in the United States ♦ Web access requires downloading of NetLauncher software ♦ Upgrading access to 28.8 Kbps speeds ♦ ISDN access available in Europe ♦ Some corporate high-speed access available ♦ Provides Spry Mosaic Web browser, allows choice of browsers ♦ $9.95 per month for three hours, $2.50 additional hour ♦ $24.95 for 30 hours monthly, $1.95 additional hour
Microsoft Network	♦ Access through Windows 95 OS ♦ Web browser available ♦ Blackbird multimedia authoring toolkit ♦ Under $5 per month for three hours, $2.50 additional hour ♦ $20 per month for 20 hours, $2.00 for additional hour
Prodigy	♦ POPs in 500 cities in the United States ♦ Mostly 14.4 Kbps access with some 28.8 Kbps ♦ Testing ISDN access ♦ Prodigy Web browser available ♦ $9.95 per month for five hours, $2.95 per additional hour ♦ $30 per month for 30 hours

The online services have an advantage because they advertise and promote their services to users and prospects, making it possible to know in advance where specific materials can be found and what the contents are likely to be. On the other hand, online services require a monthly subscription fee and surcharges for the most desirable materials.

AOL recently acquired Redgate Communications, which is a multimedia marketing organization. The objective of the company is to migrate its estimated 2.6 million users from standard GUIs to a MUI. It established its own Web server presence and provides a Web browser to users.

CompuServe developed a Web server presence and provides access to Internet for its 3.3 million users, allowing a choice of Web browsers while providing Spry Mosaic. The company also developed a multimedia companion CD-ROM updated bimonthly at the user site. It includes videos, interviews, movie clips, music, travelogue materials, and provides indirect interactivity, but lacks real-time multimedia capability.

The relatively young online service e-World of Apple Computer was designed with an MUI from the start and uses simulated "city" locations for navigation. While it is Apple-related, the company is also developing a Windows version.

Prodigy, one of the oldest online services with more than 1.6 million users, is highly consumer-oriented. It provides a Web graphical browser and launched its own Web server. This service permits advertising, and thus, is of renewed interest to those who want to promote themselves in cyberspace.

Delphi, which established text-based access to Web, is now implementing a Netscape Web browser as a main GUI for its online services and Internet access. Delphi is a relatively small service, but has been acquired by the News Corporation owned by Rupert Murdoch, and there are expectations this will change the service into a global system of significance.

GEnie, the General Electric online service, is highly technical with only 350,000 subscribers, but it is famous for its multiplayer games. While expensive, this service may become significant in the future because its video games represent some of the best in the industry.

Global Connectivity Issues

If global connectivity is important, it is necessary to ascertain if international offices of the ISP will be connected to the Internet. Only a few ISPs – CompuServe, IBM Global Network, and Sprint – currently provide such coverage. Internationally, the number of countries in which a service exists is not important, but rather how many POPs are available in the countries is of importance to the user.

This is critical because corporate users in many countries also require leased lines to the nearest POP, and prices for such facilities (controlled by state telecommunications monopolies) are considerably higher than in the United States. The widest coverage for ISPs and different types of connections currently exists in Belgium, France, Germany, Italy, Japan, the Netherlands, Norway, Spain, Sweden, Switzerland, and the United Kingdom. However, telephone carriers in most countries are also developing additional Internet access services and the availability of ISPs throughout the world is expanding rapidly.

International access to the Internet also involves creation of Web pages in different languages for different target audiences. It becomes important whether a foreign office of an ISP can provide Web server services including home page development, security, maintenance, and 24-hour monitoring for effective global operations.

Many of the larger ISPs are competing globally to provide Internet access in different countries, but these efforts are often frustrated or restricted in scope because of poor telecommunications infrastructures, local monopolies, and regulations. A major objective of U.S. ISPs establishing foreign POPs is to please their existing customers, while offering more competitive pricing to their clients by increasing the number of POPs.

Sprint is considered the dominant international Internet access provider, carrying more than 50% of international Internet connectors including countries such as Brazil, Jordan, Malaysia, and Russia. Another incentive to expand internationally is the development of voice services over Internet, which will cost considerably less than traditional telephony.

Conclusions

Access to the Web is available through ISPs and online services, but the character and quality varies widely from service to another. The main issue facing a user is to select a service provider that offers access of sufficient bandwidth to transmit multimedia content to and from the Web with an acceptable speed and minimum latency or jitter.

There are several types of Web connections available, but not all are suitable for effective multimedia transmissions. Users also need to acquire a Web browser to view multimedia contents of a typical Web home page.

There are thousands of ISPs that offer connectivity with the Web on a local, regional, national, and international basis. Most major ISPs provide high-speed links, but many low-cost local ISPs offer only dial-up or, at best, ISDN access to the Web. This is barely adequate for effective multimedia transactions.

Users should investigate ISPs to determine if their networks, Web servers, and connections to the Internet meet the requirements of proposed Web presence and multimedia content and transmission parameters.

ISPs should be evaluated with regard to Web access options, backbone topology, usage patterns, NAP connectivity, redundancy, Web server capabilities, Web hosting services, congestion, security provisions, utilization reporting, and pricing alternatives.

Web access through online services is possible, but these are not set-up to host Web pages and provide primarily low-cost, low-speed access to the Internet for small businesses and individual consumers.

Only a few ISPs worldwide provide true global coverage. The most important issue in international Web operations is to determine which ISO offers the most POPs in countries of importance to the user, and not the number of countries in which a service operates.

Chapter 5

Multimedia Browsers for the Web

No matter how sophisticated a browser may be in retrieving multimedia data, the process is often frustrating and unpredictable due to the uneven bandwidth of Internet connections, congestion, and delays at various transmission points. The greatest challenge in using a Web browser is selection of a product that displays multimedia content and includes a number of features that are preferred by the user.

Details about Web browsers on the market and their availability are maintained by BrowserWatch at:

http://ski.mskcc.org:80/browserwatch/index.html/

by Web FAQ at:

http://sunsite.unc.edu/boutell/faq/www_faq.html

by Yahoo at:

http://www.yahoo.com/Computers/World_Wide_Web/browsers/

What Is a Web Browser?

A Web browser is a very simple and transparent user application designed to display pages of the Web. Conceptually, it is similar to a window through which the user looks at the contents of the Web. A Web browser can display documents which include linked graphics, animations, audio, and video clips. Because Web browsers have been developed to support other Internet protocols they are perceived by many as the graphical GUI of the Internet.

The Web browser is an example of a client program in the C/S environment. It accepts instructions from the user and obtains information and services by transmitting requests to the Web server programs. A typical Web server is a system that can simultaneously provide such information to thousands of clients.

Web pages are hypertext documents including links to other pages, which in turn, can be linked to other multimedia objects such as graphics, images, sound bits, and video clips. When the user moves a mouse pointer across a page under browser control links, other objects are underscored or change color to alert the user additional information is available at that point. When the user selects a particular link and clicks the left mouse button, the browser immediately clears the screen and displays the new document or object to which the link referred.

Web browsers are based on HTML, which is regulated by the Web Consortium operated by the Massachusetts Institute of Technology (MIT) in Cambridge, Massachusetts. The latest formal specification is HTML Version 2.0, upon which most Web browsers are currently based. However, the consortium is already developing HTML Version 3.0, which will support such features as tables, incline figures, and customized backgrounds.

At the beginning of 1996, more than 20 major Web browsers were on the market. Some can be downloaded from the Internet, while others are bundled with applications software. Most browsers are available free of charge for trial periods ranging from 30 to 90 days, after which a fee is collected. Others are completely free.

Original Web browsers were designed to look at Web pages and their text or multimedia content. The latest Web browsers in development include many additional functions such as search engines, E-mail, and authoring systems. While some Web browsers are being developed commercially as comprehensive application development front-ends, others are integrated into specific applications software as extra features or options.

Web browsers sold as commercial products are available at a relatively low cost, ranging from $30 to $200 per user within a site license. The commercial versions of Web browsers and their prices are justified in product upgrades and maintenance because of rapid changes in Web browser specifications.

Surfing the Web means spending a great deal of time interacting with Web pages using the browser, which is why additional tools are available at the browser to assist the user in navigation and discovery. Users primarily read text, inspect images, and videos, and select links to display other documents or multimedia objects. Users may also scroll the window up or down to inspect documents that are displayed on multiple pages, return to previous pages by clicking on special buttons, and return to the home page to start a search procedure. These functions are performed frequently when surfing the Web, and the Web browser provides the facilities perform these tasks with ease.

Users browsing through Web pages may also perform other tasks for which a browser provides specific facilities. These may include entering URLs or addresses of other Web sites, searching for words, phrases or even shapes and colors, printing part of a display, reloading pages, and following links in other directions.

Most browsers also include a special feature which keeps track of frequently visited pages. Using such a list, it is unnecessary to enter the address of the page, but click on the entry and the page will be displayed on the screen. These features are called "bookmarks" or "hot lists" of a browser and can be easily expanded and modified.

Web servers come in many varieties, but there are several features all effective browsers should possess. These include compatibility with other browsers, support of other Internet services, caching pages of interest, access security, and ease-of-use. Web browsers are being developed as even more comprehensive applications development tools with authoring systems and search agents, offering a comprehensive front-end to the user of Internet.

Display Compatibility

Because Web browsers vary in quality, the same Web page does not necessarily look exactly alike when retrieved and viewed by different browsers. The single most important aspect of a Web browser is whether it displays the content exactly the way it appears on the Web server. Web browser developers may have the best intentions, but those who implement the HTML coding to develop a Web browser may not interpret all the features of HTML in the same way.

Major corporate users are seeking a Web browser display standard because they want their home pages to appear in a predictable manner whenever they are accessed. These issues will increase in importance when Web interoperability and integration come into play within electronic commerce implementations of the future.

Web browser developers are trying to include the latest HTML specifications in their browser products, but different vendors accomplish this at different times. Other developers have anticipated HTML 3.0 specifications in their latest browser versions even before this standard was finalized, while others have not been able to maintain it. It is believed that, while Web browser vendors will be racing to upgrade their products to the HTML 3.0 specifications, level HTML 4.0 specifications will already be in the works and the vicious cycle of catching up will start again. As a result, it is strategically important to select a Web browser product developed by a vendor who can afford to include all the latest specifications as soon as they are announced.

Navigability of Web Browsers

Web browsers have a basic user interface and must be integrated with other Internet capabilities. How well these features are implemented and work together in a particular browser determines its navigability.

The user interface includes the hot list or bookmarks and in some products these can be organized into a graphical "map" of the cyberspace environment of interest to the user. An associated aspect that affects navigability of a browser is the capability to customize, edit, and configure bookmarks and hot lists according to user preferences.

Good Web browsers have an interface where various Internet function options should be easy to find and include quick buttons for reaching services such as FTP, Gopher, news, and E-mail applications from within the Web interface. It is also important to include filters for selection of news by name, subject, and other characteristics.

The ease of downloading content of interest is another valuable feature. Some browsers allow downloading data in the background while the Internet search continues. Others can turn off multimedia graphics displays to accelerate the downloading process.

The Caching Feature

A Web browser with a caching feature keeps a copy of the Web pages visited by the user. If the document is required again, it need not be downloaded from the original Web server, but is simply reloaded from the cache which results in a much faster process. This feature is particularly useful for handling multimedia pages because they usually take a long time to download. A browser with a caching feature is a means of saving connect time and possible charges.

Two types of caches are used and Web browsers may include one or both types. With a disk cache feature, the browser stores the pages on the hard disk so it can be retrieved under its original URL. A memory cache performs a similar function within the RAM of the system and is very fast in reloading, but it is also expensive, particularly when large multimedia files are involved.

Depending on the browser, the amount of data cached in memory or disk can be specified by setting the maximum KBs or number of documents. Netscape browsers also provide options for verifying cached documents – an important aspect considering the fact that original Web server sources are subject to unpredictable changes. This verification can take place with specific frequencies and the browser checks the latest modification date against the cached document, which still saves time and minimizes transmission costs.

Browser Ease-of-Use

There are certain basic features in a Web browser that combine to make it an easy-to-use tool, but there is always an element of personal habit and preference that also comes into play. In general, a Web browser should provide a toolbar with icon buttons for most frequently performed functions. Although most popular browsers include this feature, not all of them do.

A cutting and pasting feature for entering URL addresses into an edit box is also a very useful and time-saving device. This allows users to directly copy a complete URL from a Web page or any document instead of typing it letter-by-letter.

Other features that assist in browsing are multiple windows for looking at different pages or for running several instances of the browser simultaneously. Some browsers also provide a means to select typefaces and fonts for all text objects, which is a useful feature but goes against the rule of compatibility because the displayed documents do not resemble the originals.

Web Browser Options

Web browsers are usually preconfigured with a home page that reflects their origin and creates a starting point for Web surfing. Users may want to start at a different Web server and should be able to change the default setting to a home page of their choosing. The browser should have a home page edit box where the URL of the desired home page can be entered.

Other options that should be easily set include user names, E-mail addresses, signature files, news server, and mail servers used by the organization. Some browsers are preconfigured with generic Web server names identifying such specific sites, but the best products should provide a means of overriding such settings.

Additional options in a browser include the ability to hide some of the components from the display and customize the appearance of the browser window. This may apply to the toolbar, edit boxes, and other buttons that provide linkages to the Web server or its directories.

Some browsers also provide means to change the appearance of Web documents with background texture, color choices, and customization of link text areas. Browsers categorize links as "active," "followed," and "inactive" using different colors, underlining or highlighting. A browser setting in some products may be overridden by Web server pages that specify their appearance regardless of the browser customization.

Another feature in some browsers is the ability to change typefaces and fonts for each HTML element on the page. The basic set-up with most browsers is a means of selecting a particular base font which is used by the browser throughout with the ability to change its size. This is a useful feature when the user wants to increase the font size in some Web pages to make it more legible.

Security Features in a Web Browser

There are a number of security features that may be present in a Web browser including authentication and encryption, SHTTP, Secure Sockets Layer (SSL), and firewall provisions. One or more of these features may be built-in to a browser and their need and effect must be assessed particularly when heavy multimedia traffic is being contemplated. The effect of security programs on latency and delays in multimedia transmissions must be taken into account.

SHTTP offers secure transactions between a user and a server as the data is entered. It is being developed by the National Center for Supercomputing Applications (NCSA) in collaboration with RSA Data Security, and is being distributed by NCSA in a manner similar to the original Mosaic Web browser. AOL, IBM, Netscape, and Spry browsers offer both SSL and SHTTP security. SHTTP seems to be the more likely alternative for international Web security because encryption used in the SSL protocol is restricted by export controls to use in the United States and Canada.

SSL protocol is a Netscape-sponsored security protocol which competes with SHTTP scheme. SSL provides encryption, authentication, and message integrity, and is targeted at the creation of secure channels for Web business transactions. Unlike SHTTP, it can also secure other Internet protocols including E-mail, Gopher, Usenet, and Telnet, while SHTTP is limited to the Web. More than 20 companies support SSL and provide SSL-enabled products. However, SSL and SHTTP protocols can coexist on the same browser.

Web browsers are so simple to use the security implications of their use are often overlooked. Most browsers, for example, can receive forms from Web servers completed by the user and sent back to the Web server. Such forms can include credit card numbers, sensitive personal and medical data, financial transactions, and other confidential corporate information. Unless the browser complies with some encryption standard, data can be easily intercepted by an enterprising hacker or corporate spy.

Web browser security capabilities may include the ability to work with a firewall through a proxy server, support of encryption standards, and specific defense mechanisms against outside attacks on corporate data.

Browsing the Web from within a secured network requires the Web browser be configured to operate through a proxy server. Most Web browsers include special features for configuring them to operate with proxy servers. There are some browsers that do not have such provisions. If secure interactions are required, this must be determined in advance before selecting a particular browser.

Web browsers work well with packet filtering in firewalls because such browsing generates many connections to Web servers across routers and gateways. In the case of proxy servers when outsiders need to access a secure network, Web browsers must be configured to support the software that permits or denies access. Other proxy servers require browser software to redirect all Web connections to the proxy server.

If a Web server does not support any security standard, a software security solution can be incorporated in a firewall. As such, it provides secure transmission between the firewall and Web servers that support the same security standard.

Web browsers are also excellent tools for launching attacks driven by hackers. It is a dangerous procedure in which the act of accepting and viewing information from the outside activates the attack. The Web browser initiates a connection with a Web server for downloading a data object, receives it, and examines the header to determine how to display it. If a specific data type is not supported by the browser, it will inform the user to save it for later access with an appropriate viewer, as is the case with many multimedia transmissions. If a Web browser can automatically invoke viewers with execution capability, this could be used to create damage to the user data files.

Web browsers can only be made more secure by including options for disabling potential dangerous features. Observers are concerned that browsers of the future can become very powerful systems and present a significant threat to security of corporate networks and databases.

Multimedia Browser Issues and Requirements

Text-based browsers can be used to retrieve graphics and sound files from a Web server, but these must be viewed or played separately using a specific viewer program. The GUI browsers can display full-color images, sounds, video, and text automatically, although this can only happen on a multimedia-capable PC platform matched with properly configured browsers.

Web pages are HTML test files resident in a server waiting for someone with a Web server to read them. When such a page is addressed by a browser, it is retrieved as an HTML file into the user computer memory where each tag is interpreted to display the page as its author intended it.

HTML tags define the formatting of the text on a page and as time progresses new versions of HTML introduce additional capabilities. HTML version 1.0 includes tags for highlighting text and for displaying images as an integral component of a Web page. Such images embedded in a Web page are known as “inline images,” however the text contained on such a page cannot be made to flow around the image. HTML version 2.0 includes all features of version 1.0 and adds forms capability, which permits acquisition of inputs from the users including edit boxes and buttons making the Web an interactive medium.

HTML version 3.0 includes all features of version 2.0 and introduces “inline figures.” These are identical to inline images, but the text can flow around them. Inline figures permit faster browsing because images can be displayed in various ways as long as a Web browser supports such specifications.

Future HTML versions are expected to include additional multimedia capabilities. They will be able to provide virtual reality (VR) simulations and audio input fields into which vocal messages can be recorded. No doubt, real-time video input will also be possible.

As a result, every Web browser is capable of displaying still images in the browser window without any special programs. In fact, Web pages are not considered complete without at least one image. However, external images, sounds, and video clips attached to a Web page require external viewers.

Matching Web Server, Browser, and User File Formats

A multimedia link on a Web page looks similar to a text link, but it must correctly specify the reference file with an extension supported by the Web browser or it will be ignored. GIF or JPEG files can be incorporated into the Web pages and are image types that can be viewed by most browsers. Specific browsers can also accommodate other image types.

For video files, the most common is Motion Picture Experts Group (MPEG) because there are viewers for this format for most platforms. Video for Windows and QuickTime are two other popular formats. There is also the .WAV format for sound files and Basic Sound format used in UNIX systems with sound players available for almost every platform. The basic problem – while a link to a sound or video clip on the Web is activated, the browser has no way of knowing if it is in a format the user computer can play.

The sound and video files on a Web server must be recognized by the Web browser and the platform to play the sounds and display video clips. Sound, graphics, and video boards in the computer must simultaneously match the Web browser formats and the Web server formats. Windows 95, which has most multimedia file formats built into the OS, is currently the best solution. Other operating systems must be enhanced with the appropriate extensions.

Not every sound or video file on the Web can be activated by every Web browser on every computer platform, and the designers of Web server contents must keep that in mind. Web server content often includes at least two formats for every audio and video clip to increase the probability that such multimedia content will be received by the largest possible number of users. The end-user who wants to ensure most audio and video materials can be received must install additional programs to handle all possible formats and then configure the Web browser to recognize those helper applications.

Multimedia files are easily integrated into Web pages by creating an anchor pointing to those files. Because those are external files, however, the browsers cannot interpret or display them, but must be configured to use external media and display such files outside the browser window. This is accomplished with additional programs, but browsers must be aware of those viewers and helper applications.

For audio, video, and external images to work with a Web browser, make certain it is configured for every type of file format expected on the Web servers likely to be visited. Browsers have Setup Configuration or Preferences screens where specific multimedia content files can be associated with viewers and helper applications. Therefore, browsers can display an image, run an auxiliary program or prompt the user to take action. The main problem in building multimedia into the Web is in selecting file formats that all types of browsers and computers will be able to recognize, process, and display.

Major Web Browsers

Web browsers are continuously being developed and improved with new features becoming available every few weeks as vendors race to incorporate the latest HTTP and SHTTP specifications. It is, therefore, imperative that users examine the latest versions of existing browsers or those being used as soon as these become available, often in beta form. Table 5.1 summarizes a number of major Web browsers available on the market today. Many more are bundled with Internet service providers as part of their connectivity packages.

Table 5.1 Major World Wide Web Browser Vendors

Browser Vendor	Product	Telephone
Booklink Technologies	Internet Works	800/819-6112
EINet	MacWeb, WinWeb	512/343-0978
Frontier Technologies	SuperHighway Access	414/241-4555
FTP Software	Explore OnNet	508/685-3300
IBM	Internet Connection WebExplorer	914/765-1900
Intercon Systems	TCP/IP Connect II	703/709-5500
Luckman Interactive	Super Mosaic	213/614-0966
MCI Telecommunications	InternetMCI	202/872-1600
Microsoft	The Internet Assistant	206/882-8080
NCSA	Mosaic-freeware	217/244-0072
Netcom	NetCruiser	408/983-5970
Netscape Communications	Netscape Navigator	415/254-1900
O'Reilly and Associates	The Mosaic Handbook	707/829-0515
The Pipeline	Internaut 2.0	212/267-3636
Prodigy Services	P-2	914/448-8000
Quadralay	WebWorks Mosaic	512/346-9199
Quarterdeck Office Systems	Project Normandy	310/314-3222
Spry	Air Series Internet-in-a-Box	206/447-0300
Spyglass	Enhanced Mosaic	708/505-1010

The GUI Web browser that was initially capable of displaying multimedia content was the Mosaic developed by the National Computer Security Association (NCSA) at the University of Illinois. Mosaic later became the prototype for most of the top commercial browsers in use. It should be one of the first examined because NCSA stays current with development of Internet tools and often its innovations are ahead of those followed in industry.

An ideal Web browser should be fast, accurate, compatible with Web server documents, and flexible with a switch to eliminate graphics to speed up Web searches. For multimedia display, a browser should allow the user to designate "helper" applications required to play sound or video. It also should be able to compile a hot list and share it with other workers. Similarly, it should be able to store URLs of at least 100 sites. A good browser should communicate with other Internet protocols and be able to display HTML codes for a page. Some analysts now believe Web browsers could become ubiquitous on PCs and may even replace operating systems at some future date.

In early 1996, Web browser users were estimated at between 5 million to 7 million people or more, which is an enormous incentive for software companies to enter the market. It is particularly attractive because many Web surfers are willing to purchase more than one Web browser viewed as an entry interface to many networked applications.

The market leaders are:

- Netscape of Mountain View, California;
- Spry, a division of CompuServe in Seattle, Washington; and
- Spyglass of Naperville, Illinois.

Industry analysts claim the market is still wide open because Internet is still in its infancy and is continuing to grow rapidly.

According to Forrester Research, Inc., sales of Web browsers are expected to increase from $50 million in 1995 to about $250 million annually by the year 2000. This is not a huge market but most Web browser vendors do not expect to reap enormous financial rewards selling or licensing Web browsers software. Browsers represent a small segment of a much larger Internet products and services industry, estimated to reach about $10 billion by the end of the 1990s.

NCSA Mosaic

The original Mosaic browser was developed at the NCSA at the University of Illinois and introduced for UNIX platforms in January 1993. A Macintosh version followed in August 1993, and a PC version in March 1994. NCSA Mosaic is extremely popular because it was one of the first GUI browsers developed for the Web. Since its emergence, NCSA has maintained the development of the product and introduced many new features including security. NCSA Mosaic was the first and is one of the few browsers that includes some security features available in proxy servers and firewalls.

NCSA Mosaic 2.0 is the latest version and allows users to conduct text-based chats, send and receive files, and make joint tours of the Web with other NCSA Mosaic users without additional software or servers. It also developed AutoSurf which enables NCSA Mosaic 2.0 to download unattended all the links on a specified Web page.

NCSA Mosaic is in public domain and is distributed free of charge for internal communications. It is in constant state of revision and offers no product support. Companies that want to acquire a license to incorporate the code in their products should contact Spyglass, Inc., which has been designated the master licensee for Mosaic products.

Netscape Navigator 2.0

Netscape browsers are unquestionably the most popular and account for more than 70% of all Web browsers in use. This is in large measure due to the shareware-like distribution policy of the company and the fact that it is a powerful tool and relatively easy-to-use. It is available for Windows, Windows 95, Macintosh, and UNIX platforms, and provides connectivity to other Internet protocols. This browser also can be simultaneously connected to several Web sites and its multithreading features allow inspection of documents before they are fully downloaded, which is valuable in handling multimedia transmissions.

The Navigator 2.0 also supports E-mail and Java scripting language, while Navigator Gold is even more powerful and includes a Java-based authoring language and "What you see is what you get" (WYSIWYG) editor for developing HTML code. The Java language also allows the use of animation in Web pages and the browser includes Macromedia multimedia authoring system. It is also compatible with Adobe Systems' Portable Document Format (PDF) and Progressive Networks RealAudio which plays back sound in realtime.

The latest Navigator versions are expected to incorporate the capability to support discussion groups based on groupware software obtained with the acquisition of Collabra Software. Netscape intends to integrate groupware technology with its browsers to challenge Lotus Notes, just as Notes is developing a Web browsing capability.

Netscape allows users to download the Navigator for a free trial period and asks for a one-time fee of $39 afterward. The company is aggressively moving to provide a series of Web applications development tools targeted at corporate IS organizations building internal Webs of intranets.

Enhanced Mosaic 2.1

Enhance Mosaic 2.1 is a browser developed as a subsequent version by Spyglass, which eventually was designated as master licenser of NCSA Mosaic. Spyglass sells its Web browser code to software developers on an original equipment manufacturer (OEM) basis and does not distribute it free of charge. Many millions of copies have been licensed to OEM resellers. It is available for Windows, Macintosh, and X-Windows on UNIX platforms. However, vendors who incorporate Enhanced Mosaic in their Web browser products may distribute it as shareware or even give it away free of charge. Spyglass licensees include FTP Software, Microsoft, CompuServe, and Corel, among others.

The Enhanced Mosaic interface can be customized and appear as a special product of the licensee, for example, as Internet Explorer of Microsoft. The Enhanced Mosaic 2.1 supports several HTML extensions including tables, image wrapping, and background colors. It also has built-in support for sound files, and separate GIF and JPEG graphic viewers. Lack of caching between sessions in early versions made it relatively slower than competitive products. It includes several encryption schemes such as CyberCash, First Virtual, and Electronic Wallet designed to secure credit card transactions across the Internet. SHTTP and SSL protocols are being added to the system.

Spry Mosaic Browsers

Spry, now the Internet Division of CompuServe, is marketing two lines of Web browsers. Mosaic in a Box is one of the first easy-to-use consumer Internet browsers. It is available from computer retailers and there are an estimated 3.5 million licensees of this product.

The company also offers Air Mosaic aimed at business and corporate users. It is similar to Enhanced Mosaic in speed and navigation but has a simpler interface. Spry is among the first to implement SHTTP and SSL security protocols and features drag-and-drop hot link features. Its browser also provides connectivity with other Internet protocols.

The company customizes its Mosaic browsers for corporations as a promotional product and believes browsers have the potential to become the next marketing vehicle. Spry Mosaic sells for $49, but it is also bundled in the Internet Office suite which costs $499.

Chameleon

This Internet connectivity suite of products contains a powerful Web browser WebSurfer bundled with 18 applications to make the Internet easier to use. It is marketed by NetManage, Inc., of Cupertino, California, for a price of $495 per user.

This browser does not support SSL or SHTTP encryption protocols, but works well with firewalls and proxy servers. It is fast in downloading and permits continuing search during the process. WebSurfer also provides access to other Internet protocols. NetManage is developing its Chameleon suite to integrate E-mail, multimedia viewing, security and search agents, and drag-and-drop object facilities.

Internet Explorer

Internet Explorer is Microsoft's Web browser based on Spyglass technology and is included as part of Windows 95 or can be downloaded from the Internet. The version 2.0 of this browser is among one of the most comprehensive and advanced browser products, but it only runs under the Windows 95 OS.

Internet Explorer 2.0 includes new functionality such as support for secure transactions, tables, multimedia, and 3-D graphics. It also provides access to newsgroups, the most powerful search engines, and animation. Its security is based on SSL protocol and RSA encryption technology. It supports Support Secure Transaction (SST) technology, an electronic payment technology jointly developed by Microsoft and Visa International. The browser works with proxy servers and corporate firewalls and is designed to preserve the original look of Web pages as they were designed by the authors.

Perhaps the most interesting aspect of Internet Explorer 2.0 to multimedia developers is the fact that it supports inline audio visual interleaves (AVIs) for embedding videos, background audio, scrolling banners, and context-sensitive menus. In addition, the browser supports inline VRML for fast viewing of 3-D objects and animations. This is the first step toward bringing interactive 3-D capabilities to the Internet. In addition, features such as progressive rendering, read-ahead mode, a multithreaded user interface, and support for HTTP make this browser one of the most responsive in the market.

It is the first browser to include the RealAudio Player which allows users equipped with multimedia PCs and voice-grade telephone lines to browse, select and play back audio or audio-based multimedia content in real-time.

Quarterback Mosaic

This is a multithreaded browser from Quarterback Office Systems of Santa Monica, California. It offers a well-designed, drag-and-drop interface and is also bundled with a suite of Internet tools. The browser features multiple history hot lists which are very easy to handle. The company is shipping an enhanced version of its browser with E-mail integration. Additional features will include multimedia viewing, security, and search agents.

Emissary

Emissary is one of the most advanced Web browsers developed by Wollongong Group of Palo Alto, California. The objective of the product is to make Internet access easy and transparent to the user. It integrates Web browsing, E-mail, news reading, file access, and interactive access into a single integrated Windows application. Users can perform all those functions from within a single application in one window from one interface. Emissary automatically determines the appropriate file formats, protocols, and applications and makes access to Internet truly transparent.

The product provides users with a single view of their networked world, whether it is a Web server in the remotest part of the world or the hard disk of their PC. Emissary is seen by some analysts as the most integrated browser package on the market. The browser provides a single file tree that keeps track of all the resources including graphics and text files. These resources can be browsed in an adjacent window and URL links can be dragged among networks, hard disk, and E-mail directories.

Superhighway Access

Superhighway Access is a complete Web browser package from Frontier Technologies of Mequon, Wisconsin. It provides access to other Internet protocols including Gopher, Wide Area Information Server (WAIS), and Telnet and can handle multimedia, E-mail, and news reader. This browser does not support SSL or SHTTP encryption schemes, but operates satisfactorily with firewalls and proxy servers. The package price of $595 is on the high side considering its relative limitations when compared with more advanced Web browsers on the market.

WebSpace VRML Browser

The first VRML browsers for the Web appeared on the market in late May 1995. These are software products for viewing 3-D worlds on the Web, but it is too early to tell if such VRML navigation tools will become popular. The WebSpace VRML browser from SGI is available at no charge, but it only supports SGI workstations running IRIX 5.3 and a special SGI customized Netscape Communications Navigator browser. The WebSpace VRML browser is being ported to other platforms including Sun Solaris, IBM AIX, and Windows NT by Template Graphics Software, Inc., and these will be released on the Web at **http:/www.cts.com/~template**.

The company is also planning to release a VRML browser version for Windows 3.1 platforms which has the largest user populations in business and consumer markets and will be a test of whether the VRML browsers will be adequate. Another venture involving InterVista Software, Inc., is also developing a VRML browser for Windows, Macintosh, and UNIX platforms. Significant VRML development is also under way at the University of Minnesota. San Diego Supercomputer Center started a Web repository for software and utilities related to VRML which provides hyperlinks to VRML documents and access to VRML-related software at **http:/www.sdsc.edu/vrml.**

Web Explorer

IBM offers a full suite of Internet tools which include Internet Connection Web servers for OS/2 Warp, AIX, OS/400, and MVS operating systems. IBM also offers a set of Web Explorer browsers for use with OS/2 Warp, Windows, and AIX operating systems. The company is also developing Lotus Notes to include a Web browser. Netscape Navigator 2.0, in turn, is incorporating groupware features in its browser. Both companies are planning to integrate groupware technology with Web browsing capability.

P-2

P-2 is the Prodigy Web browser available free of charge with the Prodigy online service. There are versions for both Windows and Macintosh. P-2 is regarded as one of the easiest Web browsers to use and its setup is comparable in capabilities to Air Mosaic or Enhanced Mosaic in terms of speed and navigation. It does not have a capability for simultaneously downloading multiple Web pages, but users are limited to the tools provided by Prodigy for Internet manipulation.

InternetWorks

InternetWorks was originally developed by Booklink Technologies and is now part of NaviSoft of Needham, Massachusetts, which is owned by AOL. InternetWorks is an integrated package of tools including a Web browsers. It is part of AOL online service, but is also available as a standalone product. The Web browser includes E-mail which allows users to receive and send mail and connect Usenet clients. It is easy to group frequently used links and there is a facility for entering URLs. The browser also provides linkage to some other Internet protocols and connects to multiple sites simultaneously.

Conclusions

Web browsers are specific client programs or user GUI interfaces for easy and transparent access to the Web resources. Many browsers provide access to other Internet protocols and there is a trend to integrate browsers with a complete set of Internet operating tools.

The most important aspect of a Web browser is its ability to reproduce on the user screen the Web server page exactly as it was originally designed by the author. Navigability of Web browsers and ease-of-use of their features are also important factors in the selection of a browser.

Other browser features becoming increasingly important are security and caching of downloaded data and their subsequent manipulation. Other options depend on user background and preferences.

For effective transmission of multimedia content to and from Web servers, it is necessary to select Web browsers that can display images, graphics, audio, and video clips within the browser window. Most browsers rely on external viewers for handling audio and video content. It is very important to make sure browsers used are configured to handle every multimedia file likely to be needed.

There are more than two dozen major Web browser vendors developing and enhancing their products at a rapid rate. As a result, it is necessary to evaluate new versions of existing browsers and new products every few weeks.

There is a trend to treat the browsers as a loss leader by numerous vendors who see much greater revenues and profits resulting from Internet applications. As a result, Web browsers are being licensed from original developers and integrated with complete Internet toolkits or operating suites of programs which include connectivity with existing networks, databases, and other corporate facilities. Several vendors are developing new groupware products which include Internet access and Web browsing capabilities.

Chapter 6

Multimedia Agents on the Web

Intelligent agents hold the promise of enabling automated, unattended searching of cyberspace and acquiring information of specific interest to the user. This interaction can be in the form of embedded expert systems, software filters or other devices and sensors lying in wait across streams of real-time data. Or, it may involve active agents electronically traveling through cyberspace, exploring static databases, and any other files accessible to them.

Intelligent agents can process more variables faster than any human being. Artificial intelligence concepts and interactive multimedia communications are the basis of these new solutions, creating the real-time interactive infrastructures that will make it work.

Intelligent agents interact and operate in the background mode, searching through files in local and remote databases. They are also capable of understanding a message from someone else and responding electronically without real-time direction from their human "masters."

The interaction between the human master and the intelligent agent takes place at the convenience of the user. Once instructions are given, the intelligent agent fulfills them until otherwise instructed. The intelligent agent is active on a 24-hour basis, thereby extending the capabilities and productivity of its master beyond that of human beings.

Agents can be programmed to specialize in specific tasks, which they will then perform in networked cyberspace until otherwise instructed. If an agent is designed to act as a researcher or librarian, it knows how and where to look for certain types of information.

Should the user want to obtain an update on a particular company, for example, the agent automatically dials a series of online databases known to contain this type of information. If more extensive information is required, the agent connects with an online service which provides access to electronic versions of newspapers, trade magazines, and newswires.

Agents can acquire pertinent information and manipulate it to make it presentable to their masters. Typically, this information is presented in the form of a customized newsletter with headlines that provide hypertext linkages to the complete sources of data. Ideally, an intelligent agent would be able to learn how to perform its tasks faster, better, and less expensively as time progresses. Most software, however, is not that sophisticated.

What Are Intelligent Agents?

Intelligent agents are software programs that perform complex routines for their human masters. Such a program resembles a human secretary or valet with whom it is possible to interact intelligently and produce concrete actions. Like a personal assistant or secretary, such a program can schedule a meeting taking into account the person's availability or respond automatically to incoming E-mail or other forms of electronic communications.

The difference between expert systems of yesterday and intelligent agents of tomorrow lies in the fact that intelligent agents are capable of working on their own. Expert systems, aside from specialized monitoring systems in the process industries, require real-time interaction of the end-user to provide advice or present a solution.

Intelligent agents operate in the background mode searching through files in local and remote databases. They are also capable of understanding a message from someone else and responding electronically without real-time direction from their masters.

Agent software can be incorporated in a variety of devices and systems including interactive networks, interactive TV, personal digital assistants (PDAs), and other handheld products.

The Expanding Cyberspace Infoglut

The demand for agent technology is driven by cyberspace's chaotic and overwhelming information overload, increasingly powerful computers, and interconnected networks spanning the globe. The recent popularity of the Internet and the Web only aggravates this situation.

Simultaneously, numerous enterprises forced to operate in an increasingly competitive global economy are significantly reducing their staffs. As a result, more work must be performed by fewer workers and the only solution is to exploit their networked PCs, putting them to work while their masters are otherwise occupied in more creative activities.

In addition, most corporate PCs are networked into LANs and WANs with growing access and facilities to surf the Web and connect to any online service at any time. These networked infrastructures are constantly in place and are becoming increasingly complex with more data and information collected and stored every day. Human beings are now unable to take advantage of all this information and require automated mechanisms to search, locate, and retrieve the data that will benefit their organizations. Intelligent agents and intelligent networks are the perceived solution for this problem.

The Developing Communications Interfaces

Intelligent agents are characteristic of the third generation of interactive client/server-based online services interfaces. These have evolved as a result of the availability of powerful PCs and workstations as user terminals, and higher speed networking and digital wireless transmission infrastructures.

Initially, online services offered relatively simple and unattractive interactive interfaces consisting primarily of character-based text with command line user controls. These interfaces demanded a certain amount of learning to understand the controls and effectively use the command language. This was also a reflection on the computer technology of a decade ago when online services were based on a mainframe host, which provided the information and performed all the associated housekeeping functions except local screen rendering and manipulation of downloaded files.

The second generation of interactive communications interfaces introduced graphics and icons to facilitate interaction with users including those who are not computer literate. This type of interface is characterized by the GUI popularized by Apple and Windows. This was possible primarily as a result of more powerful PCs and workstations capable of locally processing graphics.

The third generation of interactive communications interfaces reflects even more computing power available to the user, both locally and through the C/S architecture. This generation introduced agent-based services which involve traveling software objects that can represent the user within a network even when he or she is no longer online. These interfaces now offer multimedia interactive capabilities including voice and imaging and, in the near future, video transmissions in the form of personal mobile videoconferencing.

Agents for the Internet and the Web

Surfing the Internet can be a frustrating experience when searching for a particular piece of data or information. The Internet is so vast that identifying and locating a specific document is difficult with existing browsing software. Yet even this task seems manageable when compared to exploring collections, massive or specialized databases or extensive libraries. That task is nearly impossible and there is universal agreement that agents are probably the best solution to this problem. Otherwise, it would be impossible to explore the vast information richness of the Internet.

The Web with its Mosaic hyperlinked browsers is one method, but it is operational only within the boundaries of the Web server. There is also valuable information to be found in the numerous discussion groups, news groups, bulletin boards, and other locations that can only be accessed and evaluated by an intelligent agent.

Current search engines, also known as spiders, robots, and wanderers already have many characteristics of intelligent agents. A number of ventures are hard at work to produce an agent that will be the "killer" tool for exploring the Internet.

The Internet agents allow searching for information in many ways and offer tools to manipulate and manage the information they acquire. Table 6.2 summarizes a number of spiders, wanderers, and robots for the Internet and the Web.

Table 6.1 Spiders, Wanderers, and Robots of the Internet

Internet Spiders, Wanderers, and Robots	URL
DE-CLOD	http://schiller.wustl.edu/DACLOD/daclod
Harvest Information Discovery and Access System	http://harvest.cs.colorado.edu/
JumpStation II	http://js.stir.ac.uk/jsbin/jsii
Lycos	http://lycos.cs.cmu.edu/
NIKOS	http://www.rns.com/cgl-bin/nikos
WebCrawler	http://webcrawler.cs.washington.edu/WebCrawler/
WWW Worm	http://www.cs.colorado.edu/home/mcbryan/WWWW.html
Yahoo	http://www.yahoo.com/Reference/Searching_the_Web/

Intelligent Agent Markets to Skyrocket

The emerging market for intelligent agents is difficult to define because it consists of software embedded in various networked applications. Several implementation areas have been identified as prime environments for intelligent agents. These include electronic messaging of all categories including E-mail, personal communicators (PDAs and personal communication systems [PCSs]), user interfaces, desktop applications, workflow schedulers, information retrieval, specialized search applications, and agent development tools.

In 1994, intelligent agent-related revenues in all those categories were estimated by Ovum Ltd., to total $114 million in the United States and Europe. Specific search applications accounted for the bulk of those revenues, amounting to $70 million. This market is expected to quadruple to $453 million by 1996, with specific application still remaining the largest of its segments. By the year 2000, however, the market is expected to skyrocket by more than

3,000% to reach almost $4 billion when messaging applications will become the leading segment with revenues totaling almost $800 million. Figure 6.1 illustrates this growth, but it does not include Japan, which is also expected to become a major user of agent technologies in the future.

Figure 6.1 Agent-related Market

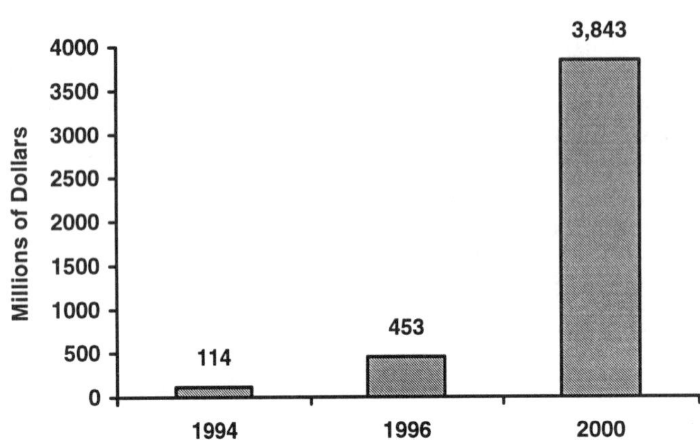

Source: Ovum Ltd.

Agents to Supervise Networking Activities

Intelligent agents are becoming particularly useful in LAN management applications which present continuous and complex interactive monitoring and problem resolution. They can assume a behind-the-scenes role of distributing software updates, gathering inventory data, and monitoring database performance. Intelligent agents are seen as the wave of the future in network management and are expected not only to alert users about network problems, but to automatically correct them.

Intelligent agents must have a knowledge base which allows them to automatically perform tasks and enables them to learn from experience. As networks become more complex and carry increased communications traffic, intelligent agents become a welcome, if not mandatory alternative to overloaded management consoles often responsible for up to 40% of total networking traffic.

Network agents monitor servers and workstations for predetermined events, they compare those events with preset thresholds, and prioritize alerts before sending them to the management console. This reduces dependence on management consoles and agents can continue monitoring the network even when the management console is not operating. Other agents monitor operating systems and databases for exceeding performance thresholds and automatically trigger predetermined corrective actions.

Agents are particularly valuable in detecting and monitoring security violations in a network and can be programmed to shut down a communications link. This is a function that may prove to be of great value in monitoring Internet and Web traffic because this is where corporate networks can become vulnerable to unauthorized penetrations.

Another valuable function performed by agents is inventory collection – particularly in networking environments that consist of thousands of users and experience frequent changes. Agent technology greatly simplifies the process of distributing software updating across such networks.

Good network management agents should remain invisible to network management and should consume less than 3% of the resources of a system in which they operate. However, agents also have their limitations and should not always be trusted in situations that require human judgment.

Handling Electronic Junkmail

One large and early problem of the cyberspace age is electronic junkmail and other transmissions that flood valuable online storage space and create an enormous search and destroy problem for those at the receiving end. Various commercial initiatives on the Web can aggravate this situation. At MIT Media Lab, an interactive agent has already been designed to screen out certain types of E-mail by removing them automatically into a file specifically designed for disposal of messages. At that stage, messages are still retrievable, but are separated from the important E-mail and can be discarded at the push of a button.

Such an agent can also learn when an E-mail message requires an immediate response by checking the sender from an organizational chart or an embedded priority list. When an E-mail message is classified as urgent and verified as such by the agent, it alerts the master that such a message has arrived and must be acted upon immediately. Agents will have to be even more sophisticated to handle videomail or multimedia E-mail of various categories because senders may want to use the ambiguity of images and videos to avoid being detected as junkmail and discarded into the electronic wastebasket.

It is conceivable the agent could automatically page or call its master if so equipped. Alternatively, the agent can inform an important executive caller that its master is traveling and make a decision whether to provide a location and contact number. This is the ultimate, real-time mobile interactivity at work and it will be relatively easy to implement within a few years.

Online Personal Shoppers

One attractive concept for an intelligent agent is its use in shopping for specific products at the best possible price. This can be applied in the corporate world and in the consumer-oriented cybermalls. These are specialized agents that research goods and services according to the tastes and requests of specific customers. As a result, online personal shoppers return information only on items a customer is likely to want to buy.

These agents are portable software objects that can communicate with specific databases to acquire information about products and prices. These agents are being developed to provide commission-based services at Web-based cybermalls and are designed to take Internet commerce to a higher operational level. Merchants who plan to offer agent access to their Web storefronts or databases are facing the need for technical modifications and additional investments.

Personal shopping agents can be more active than human shoppers and can perform their searches at all times of night and day. Such agents "learn" about the user's shopping patterns and compile such information into its own special databases. Whenever the user logs-on to a cybermall, the agent can automatically advise the shopper of which stores have added new items or sales of interest to the user.

On the other hand, customers have the choice of turning off agents' tracking capabilities and can use the agents for only anonymous shopping. In addition, agents can be made to remember special personal events such as birthdays and remind the users about these dates in time to select a gift or greeting card.

Some cybermalls are proposing shopping agents with specific personalities and areas of expertise with whom customers could maintain a dialogue about areas and products of interest. In the case of shopping for clothes, for example, shopping agents could be represented by real actors or fashion models performing those tasks for a customer.

The ultimate shopping agent is seen to be an avatar customized to represent the personality of the shopper. Such an avatar would be a compilation of agent specialist characteristics from specific areas of interest of the user. Users would through their avatars become expert shoppers on any specific item they choose to purchase.

There are, nevertheless, problems with shopping agents. Some merchants are neither eager to accept this concept nor do they wish to invest in the equipment and software required to provide such personal agent services in their stores. The other issue is technical because an attractive shopping agent requires high-capacity bandwidth that provides real-time interactive multimedia communication between the user and the agent.

How Responsible Can an Agent Be?

Intelligent agents can easily perform the tasks assigned to them or for which they were designed, and this presents no problem if these actions are controlled or owned by the user. However, agents required to roam the online services and the Internet must go through numerous gateways and checkpoints where various owners and organizations control access and collect usage fees. Agents could run up very high bills because they may not be able to discriminate when a piece of information is worth the price being asked for it.

The unresolved issue of privacy and security as it applies to individual agents that represent specific human beings in cyberspace remains. In time, an agent acquires the specific habits of its master and becomes a security risk as it interacts in cyberspace with other agents. What is needed are means of securing those habits within an agent so they cannot be deciphered and used by other people's agents.

One unanswered question about agents in cyberspace is their ability to behave responsibly. If agents behave in a manner that damages other agents or networking infrastructures, competence and liability become concerns. In effect, agents have many characteristics of a computer virus, and as such are potentially a threat to the security of cyberspace in which they operate.

Agents being developed for use with interactive Internet cybermalls and TV networks are designed to learn the user viewing patterns, entertainment preferences, electronic shopping habits, and other interests and alert the user of programs that fit the profile. That same information, however, would be invaluable to cybermarketeters or even direct mail operators. Interactive consumers are going to insist on technical and legal measures to protect their privacy.

Other issues created by intelligent agents include the right to monitor employee productivity, automatic execution of financial transactions without human intervention, and outright replacement of certain worker categories.

Topic Agents

Verity, Inc., of Mountain View, California, is the developer of the Topic software specializing in searching databases being incorporated into Web browsers and other Web application packages. Users can build custom agent profiles by supplying search criteria and locations, and the agents will probe databases on the Web identifying matches with requests.

The results of Topic Agents are annotated with relevancy ratings describing discovered documents and their URL links to Web sites where they were found. Users depend on relevance ratings to decide which sites to personally investigate. The Topic search engine produces accurate, relevance ranked results from even the simplest of queries. The company's products and services for information retrieval are used by more than 650 corporations and organizations worldwide, and by hundreds of original equipment manufacturers (OEMs) development partners who embed Topic Agent technology into their products. The Verity search engine is used in Netscape, Lotus Notes, Adobe Systems, and Microsoft products. More details can be obtained at: 415/960-7600.

Searching for Multimedia Objects Is Tough

Multimedia presents a special problem for search agents. Multimedia content in various forms including text, graphics, audio and video files is increasingly found in corporate databases and Web servers. As a result, there is a growing need for efficient multimedia data querying and manipulation products.

In conventional databases that contain mostly text and numbers, query criteria are relatively simple and can be expressed in terms of keywords, characters, dates, and numeric values. Those methods have been extended to querying multimedia data often stored in conventional database systems, but they are proving inadequate to efficiently manage multimedia data files as these accumulate in business environments.

The main problem centers around the fact that standard descriptors such as keywords or numeric values are not very precise in describing images, sounds, and video elements of a multimedia database. Different people have different perceptions of multimedia contents and even the same person may describe the same image or graphic differently, depending on the context in which it appears or is going to be used.

Thus, new visual querying techniques are being designed specifically to manage multimedia data. They are based on an image comparison approach rather than the imprecise keyword descriptive methodology.

Content-based Search Methodology to the Rescue

Initial content-based query methods have focused on manipulating image data because they are the most common multimedia files stored in databases. Sound and video files can be searched in a similar way and there is little question that such methods are already under development.

Content-based querying of multimedia data has already attracted a number of vendors to develop specific software products to implement this technology. IBM was among the first to research this area, but the most innovative approach has been taken by Virage, Inc. of San Diego, California, whose principals have participated in the early IBM research on this topic.

Virage developed a software engine that analyzes, compares, and manages graphic images that exist as Binary Large Object (BLOBs) in any database. The Virage technique employs four basic image features including color, composition, texture, and shapes to query a multimedia database. In addition, each of those features can be further queried according to various "primitives" on a global or local image basis. The Virage engine includes a collection of various primitives for that purpose, but it also allows developers to add customized primitives for even finer querying of the databases.

The Extended Virage product also provides convenient image processing functions for scaling, cropping, contrast, and other image manipulation activities. The Virage engine can be used with Relational Database Management Systems (RDBMSs), Object Databases (ODBs), and other database forms – enabling users to define their content-based queries with a drawing tool to sketch an example of the image they seek. In addition, users can define multimedia objects within an image indicating a desire to find similar objects in the database.

The Virage queries also can be influenced by assigning weights to the basic search criteria indicating which are the most significant to the user. The Virage search returns thumbnail images ranked according to a similarity factor ranging from 0.0 to 100.0, with the best matches appearing first and ranked nearest to the 0.0 rating. Users can also control how many matches they are willing to inspect.

The Virage engine is written in C++ and is available for Windows, Macintosh, and SGI platforms. It also can be recompiled for specific UNIX operating systems. The current product supports only images, but it is being extended to handle video content in the future. The object-relational hybrid database vendor Illustra Information Technology of Oakland, California is actually licensing the Virage engine as a basis for its Visual Intelligence System database product.

IBM's San Jose Laboratories in California were, in fact, the first to develop the Query by Image Content (QBIC) technology. The company recently integrated it into the IBM Ultimedia Manager for OS/2. IBM also announced Relational Extenders for DB2 which are an extension of the QBIC approach to that product line.

Harvest

The Harvest search tool is an integrated set of software to gather, extract, organize, search, cache, and replicate relevant information throughout the Internet. Harvest can be instructed to "digest" information in many different formats and produce customized reports.

Harvest is a Web search system continuously under construction. It is a project of the Internet Research Task Force Research Group on Resource Discovery and is supported by the Advanced Research Projects Agency (ARPA), the U.S. Air Force, National Science Foundation (NSF), Hughes, and Sun Microsystems.

Harvest consists of an integrated set of tools designed to operate across the Internet. It is a significant attempt to provide a comprehensive and flexible Internet search system and is expected to become one of the most powerful Internet search tools. Details of this product are available at: **http://rd.cs.colorado.edu/harvest/.**

Lycos

Lycos is an example of an agent that scans the Web, Gopherspace, and FTP archives every day, and creates a database of all the Web pages it uncovers. It also automatically updates the index of database every week. The Lycos site was developed at the Carnegie Mellon University and contains indexed searchable references to more than 5 million Web documents.

Lycos has a automated exploration routine which regularly searches Web pages to locate new or changed documents and develop their abstracts which include Web page title, headings, subheadings, 100 most significant words, and the first 20 lines of text. It also provides size counts in the form of number of words and bytes. These attributes can be searched in a quasi-Boolean way and are displayed according to relevancy rankings. Lycos can be reached at: **http://lycos.cs.cmu.edu/.**

WebCrawler

The WebCrawler searches the Web for documents examined and whose brief content descriptions are then accumulated in an index. WebCrawler operates by traversing the Web, either building such an index for later inspection or it can search on a real-time basis for a specific query. The WebCrawler database can be searched by keywords which will be matched against contents of Web documents, not only titles and URLs.

The result of a search is a list of document descriptions with an evaluation number indicating how well the document matches the search terms defined by the user. These are rated from 1,000 for perfect match down to 0, which denotes the least acceptable match arranged in descending order. Analysis of such a list brings to mind other keywords that may improve the process in the next round. In addition, WebCrawler can be instructed to examine specific home pages or documents if the URLs of such items are known.

WebCrawler, created in January 1994 at the University of Washington as a Web robot, is now owned by AOL and is among the best-known search engines. The product searches unexplored links in documents whose indexed contents meet search criteria defined by the user with forms-based Web browsers. The system responds to about 2 million queries every week. It is available at: **http://Webcrawler.cs.washington.edu/WebCrawler/Home.html**.

Regional Engine WebServer Software Developer's Kit

Regional Engine WebServer Software Developer's Kit (SDK) is a search agent product from InText of San Francisco, which allows users to present naturally worded queries. The software provides a list of discovered documents with relevancy rankings and summaries. It also includes unique HTML authoring and hyperlink features that permit an HTML page to be downloaded with all the links which can be used to directly connect with Web sites of interest from the user's browser. More details about the agent is available from InText at 415/391-5290.

The Uncertain Searcher's Agent

One of the more exotic agent-based technologies comes from Architext Software of Mountain View, California. The Uncertain Searcher's Agent is concept-based and locates relevant information even if the user is unsure of what he or she is seeking. The product will locate documents with similar content, context and generate abstracts, subject groupings, and automatic hypertext links to the Web sites where these exist. More details about this search engine from Architext Software at 415/934-3611.

What Is IBM Doing on the Agent Scene?

IBM is also involved with the search agent concept and has established an InfoMarket Search Service that searches a wide variety of databases on the Internet. Special agent software allows users to search the Web and in-house databases simultaneously with the same query. The service controls searches by concept, example, text, patterns or other common methods supporting a number of database environments including Topic agents. The problem with such an approach is that Web servers must have special InfoMarket resident agents to recognize queries from users.

The General Magic Story

General Magic of Sunnyvale, California, is seen as a leading supplier of agent development technology. The company developed Telescript and Magic Cap which are a scripting language and ROM-based OS being licensed to manufacturers of communications devices. The venture is backed by Apple, Fujitsu, and Motorola. The Magic Cap software environment is a platform for communications applications and a basis for personal communicators. The OS includes voice, fax, E-mail communications modes, and other features for managing personal information.

The GUI represents real-world objects on a screen with familiar images of items such as a telephone, mailbox, postcard, filing cabinet or a card file. Touching the images leads to the services represented by those images and can be used interactively to communicate or transact business. This agent-based OS is being used in personal communications systems such as Motorola Envoy and Sony Magic Link.

Telescript is a futuristic communications language with artificial intelligence which includes agents that can be deployed into cyberspace to gather information, negotiate deals, and perform business transactions. It is designed for interactive use with online services providing users the ability to carry messages or acquire data and information from cyberspace. Using Telescript, a client computer or communications device sends an agent to a server where Telescript services are installed. The agent acts on behalf of the sender. Once the connection is established, the two computers can interact independently of the networks. An agent in the Telescript environment can travel from the personal "home" communications device or computer, across a network to a directory. It will then locate electronic addresses of interest and move on to those locations to search and retrieve information or data.

General Magic wants to put its agent technology into Web servers – a change in the company's strategy, which originally conceived the intelligent agent technology to assist mobile workers in communications across public networks.

BargainFinder from Andersen Consulting

Andersen Consulting, a major systems integrator and management consultancy, is developing an intelligent agent for the Web known a BargainFinder. Initial testing involves searches through databases of online music CD servers to locate availability and prices for any CD title selected by the user. This is an initial project of Andersen Consulting in developing agent technology. The company is experimenting with effects agents may have on commodity trading markets. BargainFinder runs on Sun Microsystems Sparc-10 servers and can be accesses at: **http://www.ac.com**.

Agent Technology Suppliers

Several new ventures have emerged to develop agent technology products and services. Aside from intelligent agent products for searching databases, the Internet, and network management agents, other ventures are developing languages, operating systems, and development tools for the design and operation of agents in online environments. Table 6.1 presents a list of major agent technology ventures and their products.

Table 6.2 Major Agent Technology Ventures and Products

Company	Agent Technology Products
Beyond, Inc. Burlington, Massachusetts	Beyondmail can be taught to filter, sort, prioritize E-mail communications by sender or topic
Charles River Analytics Cambridge, Massachusetts	Open Sesame! Recognizes patters and asks if user wants it automated - an OS enhancement for creating agents
Edity Santa Clara, California	Development software for creating and training agents
First Virtual Holdings nsb@nsb.fv.com	safe-Tel is an agent development language
General Magic Sunnyvale, California	Telescript communications language with agents Magic Cap OS on ROM
Quasar Knowledge Systems Bethesda, Maryland	Agent Object System - software based on Smalltalk agent development tools
Sandpoint Corporation Cambridge, Massachusetts	Hoover - network search agent works with Lotus Notes
Presearch, Inc. Fairfax, Virginia	Pathfinder - an intelligence analysis system for finding, using, and sorting WWW sites and databases
Verity, Inc. Mountain View, California	Topic Agents - watchers, searchers and analysts Provides agent development tools for publishing and retrieving information online and on WWW. Used in Lotus Notes and Netscape browser

Conclusions

Agents are software programs that represent the user in interactive cyberspace, operating across the Internet and within networks and databases as robots.

Various forms of intelligent agents exist and are being applied in such areas as E-mail, network management, and searching large databases on the Web and the Internet. Consequently, a new industry is developing of specialized companies that create new agent languages, operating systems, and applications.

Intelligent agents are also being used to develop interactive multimedia online service networks that can handle users with various online and wireless devices.

Because the activities of an agent are similar in nature to those of a computer virus, there is also concern about responsibility and liability when agents misbehave and damage other agents or networking infrastructures.

Chapter 7

Creating a Multimedia Presence on the Web

The Web is not only an idea whose time has come. It is a concept that fulfills the ever-present corporate need to communicate, display new products and achievements, promote new services, and do it continuously under exclusive and direct control.

The Web is a new marketing environment that cannot be ignored whether it becomes a profitable undertaking in itself. As a result, corporations are rushing to develop Web sites so compelling thousands, hundred of thousands, and even millions of Web surfers will be drawn to it.

This goal presents a challenge to corporate Web site developers who must conceive, develop, and maintain Web pages that are interesting, provide something of value, and will repeatedly attract visitors. In addition, the Web pages must be directed to users with elementary computer skills and Internet users who do not have or cannot yet afford high-speed connectivity to the Internet for downloading multimedia applications. Competitive pressures may suggest elaborate, multimedia-rich Web pages winning artistic and design awards, but these pages must also be accessible to the largest possible user populations to maximize their marketing value to the sponsoring organization.

This is the major challenge to the corporate Web site developers and the growing community of Webmasters responsible for corporate Web sites on a daily basis. They must acquire and practice new skills, giving them an advantage in planning Web presence, presenting multimedia information, and using graphics, color, and other features associated with superior Web page designs.

What the Home Page Should Be

The home page of a Web site is the introductory page that identifies the sponsor, contains the corporate logo, a brief description of the company, and provides navigational links to other related pages. These pages, in turn, contain background information, product and service descriptions, press releases, supporting images, audio and video clips, and links back to the actual home page.

There are home pages of individuals and groups representing social, religious, ethnic, and political orientations. Some of those home pages are unusual to say the least, often non-conformist, bizarre, occasionally vulgar and offensive. Clearly, these are not likely to be business Web sites or presentations, but it is important to be aware of their existence and the potential of someone creating unwanted links. The important point to remember is that a home page on the Web – whether an intricate, expensive, interconnected corporate site or a simple single level individual home page – will take up the same amount of space in a Web browser window, leveling the field for all participants.

Seeking the Best Interface Design

When competing with a multitude of Web sites and home pages, it is first necessary to observe the basic principles of good interface design. This is how a company ensures it starts with the advantage already enjoyed by successfully launched Web sites or servers.

The Web provides access to the best sites and even details of how those home pages were constructed. It will benefit any Web site developer to create a hot list of such sites and review their home pages to determine to what degree they conform to the rules of good interface design.

There are a number off factors of home page interface design that must be considered. These include content, clarity of the design, use of color, graphics, audio, and video materials. Moderation and time-proven aesthetics in the use of these factors combine to contribute to a compelling home page design. The impact of those factors on home page interface design are summarized on Table 7.1.

Table 7.1 Home Page Interface Design Criteria

Home Page Design Aspect	Description and Comments
Content	♦ Identify as a home page by layout ♦ Include company logo at the top ♦ Use professional appearance
Clarity	♦ Limit amount of information on page ♦ Generous use of blank space ♦ Use distinct page sections ♦ Outline format only for text ♦ Uncrowded by unnecessary links ♦ Separators between sections
Use of Color	♦ Stay with conventional meanings ♦ Yellow for grabbing attention ♦ Red for warning or danger ♦ Green for moving ahead and success ♦ Royal colors for positive reactions ♦ Avoid adverse color combinations
Audio and video	♦ Audio clips behind optional links ♦ Video clips behind optional links ♦ Full home page message without audio and video

As far as content is concerned, the home page should be immediately and unambiguously identified as such. One of the best identifiers of home pages is the corporate logo with several statements outlining the corporate mission and activities – also giving the reader with an icon link to additional details on the topic. The key to an aesthetically pleasing home page interface design is its professional appearance that immediately conveys to the reader it is a home page of a serious business entity.

This is best achieved by a clear home page display, which usually depends on limiting the amount of information. The corporate logo should stand out clearly at the top of the page without being crowded or surrounded by text or navigation buttons. Generous use of white space is probably the best, although many designers feel blank space is a waste of valuable resources.

This could not be farther from the truth. A home page crowded with a lot of text and links is more likely to be taken as a lower level background page and overlooked. This may become particularly significant when electronic agents start evaluating home pages based on ratios of text, blank spaces, and images as they combine to present a desirable combination.

Home page clarity is also helped by displaying an outline format of text and convenient separation between logo, outline, and navigation sections. Home pages should be efficient on all counts and particularly uncrowded with unnecessary links.

The use of color is another aspect that should be given serious attention in design of the home page. Whether consciously or unconsciously, people react in specific ways to certain colors. Yellow for example, is generally used to capture attention, while red signifies danger or a warning of potential unwanted consequences. Green is universally accepted as the color of release or correct response and should always be used in that context.

There are also certain color combinations that, for some reason, elicit either positive or negative reactions among viewers. Depending on the objective of a home page, the use of such color combinations should be carefully checked. More importantly, is necessary to investigate how colors designed into the home page at the Web server will appear on a variety of end-user PCs and workstation screens.

The best color combinations, known as the "royal colors," include wine red, blue, and gold because they blend extremely well in various proportions. In contrast, combinations of dark colors such as blue, red, black, and green tend to clash and invite negative reactions.

Colors, of course, do not exist on their own, but underscore parts of text, graphics or images. Effective graphics are excellent attention grabbers and most corporate logos are designed with that objective in mind.

While graphics – particularly animated graphics and videos – provide true multimedia content in a home page, the Web site designers must remember many users do not have high-speed connections to the Web and rely at best on telephone lines with a 28.8 Kbps modem. Downloading a large graphic image at the very beginning of a home page could prove to be very time-consuming and frustrating to the user. It would be practically impossible to use audio or video or other high resolution images under the circumstances.

The best home page design should use icon-sized graphics and images rather than their full-sized versions. However, for the benefit of those users who have adequate high-speed connections or are willing to wait for downloading of such multimedia objects, these icons should also appear as links to their full-sized versions. Many Web home pages are designed in such a way.

This also holds true for personal home pages of employees or individuals who want to include their digitized photographs at the start of their home page. A thumbnail version of or an icon indicating such an image with an immediate optional link is preferred to the actual full-sized image at the outset.

This is even more important when dealing with audio and video clips. Thumbnail images are mandatory for the home page and representative icons for proportional full-sized displays are the best solutions. This in itself presents a challenge because the home page must appear as a professional compelling presentation based primarily on limited legible text, colors, layout, and combination of small graphics, icons and very short thumbnail videos.

Storyboarding the Web

The objective of storyboarding is to plan in advance the home page, the links, the various levels of background, detail, multimedia pages, and the navigation between them all. This is best done with pencil and paper identifying each page involved and the information flow from each page to every other page. Typically four to five levels can handle company and product information, related product categories, specific product lines, specification pages providing full details, images, photographs, videos of usage, installation, endorsements, and order forms.

Figure 7.1 A Sample Web Storyboard

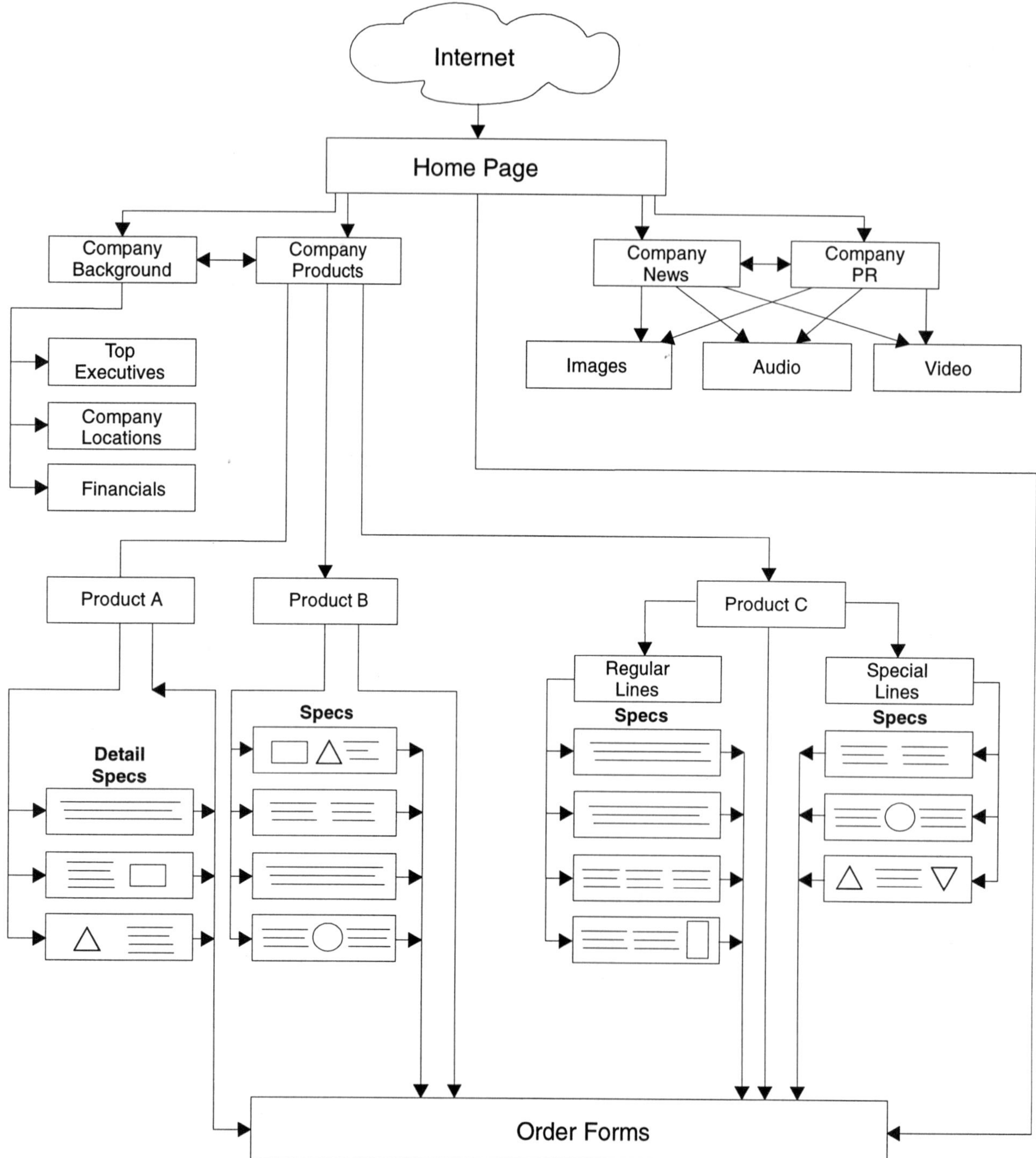

A storyboard for the Web site is a flow chart starting at the home page and showing the proposed logical links from page to page. At this stage, it is not necessary to design the individual pages because the focus should be on navigation. Some links such as those provided to return to the initial home page are always at the bottom of each page and need not be defined.

There are some support pages that may be quite lengthy and need to be scrolled by the user. For this type of page, a good interface design should provide special links, taking a user directly to the section of interest within a long page. Any means of increasing the user access speed to information enhances the overall design. In such lengthy pages, local navigation may include buttons in several sectors to allow a quick return to the top of the page and to the home page itself.

Using HTML

Once basic navigation between the home page and the supporting pages is determined, one must design the page content including its textual and multimedia elements. The concept of hypertext becomes important at this time with keywords, icons, and image areas becoming links to related information wherever it may exist on the Web.

The designer of a Web home page is not limited to pages or files created for the Web site or available in corporate databases. Every document on the Web is now available to enhance the functionality of Web pages. Too many links to off-site Web pages could confuse and frustrate the user. As a result, it is necessary to exercise restraint and good judgment in selecting links to other Web sites.

To accomplish that linkage, it is necessary to employ a common standard for representing specific elements of a document: HTML. Consider HTML as text of a document that contains special instructions that indicate to a Web browser how the document is to be displayed.

This is accomplished through the use of markup codes or tags, which are, in fact, words or symbols enclosed in standard less than < and greater than > characters. Aside from these tags, the use of HTML also involves two special tags indicating the beginning and the end of a document.

The HTML concept had its origins at IBM which created the General Markup Language (GML) for identifying commonly occurring elements in a document. In 1986, the International Standards Organization (ISO) defined a markup language – its ISO 8879 publication known as Standard Generalized Markup Language (SMGL) – for creating standardized documents. SGML actually defines many different types of documents, one of which is hypertext. HTML is a subset of SGML used to define hypertext documents. Within the Web environment, HTML is often used to define hypertext documents and the markup language used to create them.

At the beginning of 1996, four versions of HTML were released and a fifth version is being developed. Each new version is a subset of the previous one. Table 7.2 presents a summary of HTML versions in existence, those being developed, and those expected in the future. The biggest problem Web-related software developers face is including the latest HTML standards in their products and ensuring browsers and servers are developed to include the same HTML standards. From the view of the developer, the best strategy is to seek those products that provide the means to upgrade their Web development or navigation tools to keep up with the latest HTML versions as they are released.

Each new HTML version provides additional functionality without changing the way the tags work in previous versions. Web browsers updated to interpret the latest HTML version can also understand documents developed using earlier versions of HTML. By the same token, earlier Web browsers that have not been updated may not be able to completely interpret documents tagged with the latest version of HTML.

Creating an HTML Document

An HTML document contains a head section and a body section, each of which includes a number of elements. Some HTML documents may also contain a prologue. Table 7.3 summarizes the major sections of an HTML document. The prologue is a string of text at the very beginning of an HTML document that informs future browsers which HTML version was used to create the document. Prologues are expected to become much more important with the introduction of 3-D browsers, 3-D Web, and video pages. Use of HTML version 3.0 does not yet require use of prologue in HTML document development.

Table 7.2 Summary of HTML Versions

HTML Version	Major New Features
Version 0	♦ Includes original SGML features for defining hypertext documents ♦ All Web browsers must support HTML Version 0 to work with the Web ♦ Version 0 includes about 30 basic HTML codes
Version 1	♦ Includes all Version 0 features and adds nine new tags for highlighting text and displaying images integral part of a Web page ♦ New tags include bold text, italics, teletype, and typewriter fonts, underlined and emphasized text, and others; inline images provide initial multimedia content, but text cannot flow around these images
Version 2	♦ Includes all features of Version 1 ♦ Additional support includes forms which can accept user inputs that make the Web a truly interactive medium ♦ Most browsers support Version 2 HTML
Version 3	♦ Also known as HTML+ ♦ Supports all features of Version 2 and adds tags for rendering tables and inline figures on Web pages; inline figures allow text to flow around the image; also supports mathematical equations and formulas and can dynamically customize browser menus and toolbars from and HTML document ♦ Not all browsers support Version 3 yet
Version 4	♦ Unofficial developments are under way by Web Consortium and individual software developers; new features are expected to include blinking tags, virtual reality documents, audio input fields, and eventually direct video input ♦ For latest ideas and proposals under development contact: http://www.w3.org/ http://www.lcs.mit.edu

Table 7.3 Organization of an HTML Page

Page Section	Description of Elements in Section
Prologue	♦ Not a mandatory element ♦ Initial line of text on page ♦ Identifies HTML version of document ♦ Becomes more important with multimedia content of Web pages

Page Section	Description of Elements in Section
Head Section	♦ Defines overall HTML document attributes ♦ Defines TITLE element ♦ Defines BASE element ♦ Required for good page design ♦ Includes LINK elements ♦ Includes BANNER elements ♦ Can include ISINDEX, META, NEXTID, RANGE, and SPOT elements
Body Section	♦ Includes headings ♦ Uses the paragraph element ♦ Uses anchors for links ♦ Breaking lines ♦ Horizontal tabs ♦ Rule lines ♦ Includes several list varieties ♦ Accepts preformatted text
Character Attributes	♦ Used for formatting sentences, phrases, words or individual characters ♦ Font-style elements ♦ Information-type elements

Nevertheless, the use of prologue is recommended because most current Web browsers cannot identify the HTML version used in coding a particular document and simply ignore misunderstood tags. If a prologue exists, some of the latest browsers may be able to identify the HTML version in use and warn the user about their capability to interpret it.

Adding Mark-up Tags

The head section of a Web page begins with a <HEAD> and ends with a </HEAD> tag. It identifies the overall HTML document attributes and its two most important elements – the TITLE and the BASE elements.

The TITLE is the element displayed in the bar of the window in which the Web browser is operating. If a browser is iconized or minimized, the title of the Web pages appears under the icon used to represent the browser. The TITLE is set in HTML by including the text between <TITLE> and </TITLE> tags.

Although a title is a helpful element to have on a page, it is not mandatory. Web browsers may display URL address of file names instead or the word "untitled." On the other hand, the existence of a title enhances the identity and professional appearance of a Web page.

The BASE element in the HEAD section defines a starting point for all linked references in the HTML page. It is an absolute reference to the HTML document created and is particularly important for keeping track of external files typical of multimedia images, audio or video components of a Web page.

The LINK elements of the HEAD section are used to define relationships between HTML pages, making it possible to include "next" and "previous" buttons on a page. The tag for this element is <LINK> and it does not have a terminator because it applies to the entire document. Relationships are defined with REL attributes and with HTML 3 LINK elements. They also can be used to define a BANNER for the HTML document. A BANNER is a fixed part of a page that remains on the screen when it is being scrolled and is a requirement for good Web page design.

Some Web browsers provide the means to customize the appearance of Web pages by changing the display fonts on the user platforms. This changes the appearance of the Web pages from their original design, however, which the authors intended to be seen by the user. In cases of marketing and promotional pages, this may could lead to undesirable effects and misunderstandings.

Other HEAD elements such as ISINDEX inform the Web browser that it is an interactive page that accepts input from the user. The META element allows embedding information into HTML page for which an extraction procedure must be developed at the Web server. The NextID element is an automatic tag assigning a unique ID number to HTML documents. RANGE and SPOT elements are used to identify and highlight results of a search.

In the body section, headings represent words or phrases highlighted to stand out as titles of sections or paragraphs. HTML includes six standard levels for headings ranging from large, bold centered characters to bold, indented normal-size characters. The heading level is specified in text with <Hx> tag where x = 1, 2, 3, 4, 5 or 6 depending on heading level selected.

When designing text headings on Web pages, keep in mind that browser developers interpret HTML specifications individually for all elements of HTML. As a result, headings on the same page may look different when viewed by different Web browsers. The solution is to check the Web page HTML coding with several of the most popular browsers and adjust it to look as originally intended. This adds to the cost of development, but it is insurance that most users will see what the company wants them to receive.

The paragraphs in the body section were originally indicated by the <P> and </P> tags, but it this was redundant. Now the <P> tag at the beginning of a new paragraph following a blank line is used. Hypertext references can be placed anywhere within a designated paragraph. Line breaks denoted by <BR> tags provide additional control over paragraph appearance. Browsers generally ignore the standard tab character in text. In HTML tabs can be used with <TAB> element or with INDENT attribute to obtain the same effect.

A very useful element in the body section is the horizontal line which is known as Horizontal Rule with the tab <HR>. Newer versions of some browsers can display lines with different thickness and lengths using SIZE and WIDTH attributes. Lines between sections of a Web page are extremely useful to clarify the display for the reader.

Another very valuable feature in the body section are various types of lists. Three list categories exist in HTML:

- Ordered;
- Unordered, and
- Definition lists.

Ordered lists include numbered line items starting with the default value of one, but with HTML 3 any number can be the first number. Unordered lists are simply bulleted line entries. Directory and menu lists are variations of the unordered lists for short line items intended for columnar displays.

The definitions list is also known as the glossary. These lists consist of the word to be defined and the definition itself. Definition lists use two separate tags to accomplish this effect.

Another feature in the body section is the Preformatted Text. This function is designed to ensure that a Web browser renders text precisely the way it appears on the original HTML document. This is accomplished by the use of <PRE> and </PRE> tags that force the browsers to treat any space and special characters literally, and preserve all existing lines and relative positions of all the characters appearing in that text.

HTML elements describe the appearance of text on a Web page, but there are also character-level attributes available with those elements to further format sentences, phrases, words or even individual characters. These character-formatting devices include font-style and information-type elements. These are the attributes that can define boldface, italics or underlined styles. Information-type elements provide logical emphasis of letters or words within a phrase.

Adding Graphics, Voice, and Video

The real value of Web home page is realized when multimedia elements can be included, but this is not as simple as it appears. Images and graphics are supported by HTML 1 and are known as "inline images." These are embedded on a Web page in a manner similar to a line of text, but the text cannot be made to surround them and follows in the next line below the image. This aspect is addressed in HTML3 by "inline figures." These are basically the same as inline images, but text can flow around them.

When incorporating multimedia elements into Web pages such as images, graphics, sound or video, it is important to remember that their integration in a Web page has little to do with HTML as such. As a result, integrating multimedia is relatively easy. The creation of an anchor pointing to a multimedia file is the only necessary element. The creation of an attractive and compelling multimedia file is another matter and may turn out to be quite difficult.

Anchoring multimedia files is accomplished with an <A tag followed by the address of the linked graphic, audio or video file. The problem with this

arrangement is that most browsers cannot interpret or render multimedia files, and users must configure their particular browser and hardware platforms to receive the multimedia content in its entirety.

An inline image is embedded in the Web page with the <IMG> or <FIG> tag. Instead of using such tags, an anchor can be used with headline reference and the address of an image in GIF or JPEG file format. Such a Web page will appear with a link to the image file which is external to the HTML page itself. It can be retrieved by a user who has a Web browser configured to invoke exterior viewers installed on his or her system to view the image. The idea is to inform the user of the existence of an image and provide an option to view it with the appropriate hardware and software facilities.

To provide the reader with some idea of how the image may look, a thumbnail image can be substituted as an alternative at the anchor point. Readers with a relatively fast 28.8 Kbps modem or an ISDN connection might be willing to wait for a few seconds to download such an image and on seeing it might be tempted to download the full-size version at some other time. Another alternative is to include a small graphic icon indicating the existence of the image and providing an alternative link to it.

In some cases, a Web pages may provide a list of images supporting presentation pages. Each entry on such a list is a direct link to a complete image and the user may choose which images to view and in what particular sequence.

Incorporating Sound

There are no HTML inline sound facilities, thus, any sound files anchored to Web pages must be treated as external files. There are sound formats supported by various operating systems including Windows, UNIX, Macintosh, and others. The best course of action when sound is to be included in the Web pages is to design sound files that can be handled by the largest number of user platforms or make sure alternative sound files are using audio links such as .AV, .WAV, .SND, and .AIFF.

Sound file formats must be converted to ensure these alternatives are available on the Web page. The two sound formats that are most often used are .WAV for Windows and .AIFF for Macintosh platforms – two formats that should be made available to the user. If original sound clips exist in another format, it is necessary to convert them to the most popular formats being used on the Web pages.

Linking a sound file is accomplished by creating an anchor with the address of the audio file. In case of alternative sound files, each will be created with a separate anchor and is often identified with an icon indicating the size of the file. This gives the user an idea of the amount of time it will take to download the file using the current equipment and connections.

Video on the Web

Video clips on Web pages are handled in a very similar manner to audio clips – creating anchors with addresses to one or more popular video file formats of the same video clip. The three most popular video formats include Video for Windows, QuickTime, and MPEG. The latest MPEG-2 video compression standard is very powerful and its corresponding decompression, which handles audio and video simultaneously, requires very fast hardware decoders and PC platforms.

Design of MPEG-2 video into Web pages should only be included if there is a reasonable expectation visitors to this particular Web site will be equipped with powerful graphical workstations. This is not an unreasonable expectation when the Web site represents a film studio or an advertising agency showing off its commercials developed for its clients.

When an original video clip is to be included on a Web page, it must first be recorded and digitized. The problem is that this may require a camcorder and a video capture system, which often results in digital video files in a proprietary format unlikely to be supported by the equipment of most users. Conversion into one or more of standard video formats such as AVI, QuickTime or MPEG will resolve this problem. It is important to make sure there is software on the market that will make such conversion possible before selecting the video board.

There are also Web sites that provide information about how to integrate movies and video clips into Web pages. These can be reached at:

http://www.io.org/~mbelli

or

http://www.el.dorado.ca.us/~homeport/white_paper_loc.html

Luring Customers to the Web

No matter how well designed the Web site may be with regard to content, navigability, and aesthetics, there is still the problem of locating it on a Web server and attracting the largest possible number of visitors. A corollary to this issue is, of course, the need for a means to precisely measure the demographics of the visitors and a capability to assess the impact of multimedia content on their decisions.

The most important factor in establishing a Web presence is to make sure it site is accessible 24-hours a day, 365-days a year. To do that, acquire a permanent corporate connection to the Internet or rent Web server space from an ISP with a permanent Internet connection whose facilities operate on a 24-hour basis.

In selecting a Web page hosting enterprise – whether it be an ISP or a firm specializing in hosting Web pages for third-parties – a number of factors must be considered. Cost of operations is clearly important, but must be evaluated relative to services provided. Most vendors have their own pricing structures. There are monthly and annual contracts with rates differing according to size of company, storage space required, features selected or bandwidth consumed by the visitors accessing the Web site.

When a Web site design is completed and a Web server is found, it is necessary to inform the Internet community about a new Web site and its address. This is done by listing the site in one or more Web directories, including the address on home pages of Web browser developers and ISPs "What's New" links, posting announcements on Usenet newsgroups, and subscribing to Web mailing lists. In addition, conventional advertising and public relations announcements are often made directing all publics to the new URL on the Web.

The Web directories are among the most effective means of attracting attention because most include a "What's New" section and provide linkages to a new Web site. Although Web directories cover all conceivable subjects, many include business categories where a listing can be very effective. Companies can add their listing to an existing directory by completing an electronic form. Most of those listings are implemented free of charge. Table 7.4 provides a summary of some of the best-known directories on the Web and their addresses.

Table 7.4 Major Web Directories

Directory Name	Description and URL Address
ALIWEB	Online form to register with this spider at http://web.nexor.co.uk/aliweb/doc/register_form.html
BizWeb	Online registration form on the home page at http://www.bizweb.com/InfoForm/infoform.html
CERN	Information about setting-up Web servers, netiquette, and a page describing registration forms at http://info.cern.ch.
Directory of Directories	Maintained by InterNIC offers two levels of entries free and paid; contact through E-mail: admin@ds.internic.net
EINet	http://www.einet.net
Internet Business Directory	Largest provider of corporate product and service information o the Internet; use E-mail application for listing at http://ibd.ar.com
Lycos	This is an Internet spider which records new Web sites; to register, complete form at http://fuzine.mt.cs.cmu.edu/mlm/lycos-register.html
Mother-of-all BBS	Hierarchical subject-based directory with online entry forms available at http://www.cs.colorado.edu/home/mcbryan/public_html/bb/ad b.html
NCSA What's New Page	Copies of Mosaic include automatic pointer to this page wit online forms available at http://www.ncsa.uiuc.edu/SDG/Software/Mosaic/Docs/whats new-form.html
Open Market Commercial Sites Index	Online submission forms for companies, institutions, and organizations at http://www.directory.net/dir/submit.cgi
Virtual Yellow Pages	http://www.imsworld.com
Whole Internet Catalog	http://www.gnn.com
WWW Virtual Library	Subject-oriented index of Web sites at http://info.cern.ch/hypertext/DataSources/bySubject/Maintain ers.html
World Wide Web Worm	WWWW is an index of Web sites with registration form available at http://www.cs.colorado.edu/home/mcbryan/www.html#new
Yahoo	Online subscription forms require category definition for listing available at http:/www.yahoo.com

When announcing the appearance of a new Web site on Usenet newsgroups or a mailing list, developers are advised to first spend several days reading typical announcements on those services. There are unwritten protocols followed by those communities which must be studied in detail. In the final analysis, however, it is the superior content, publicity, and a sufficient budget to maintain and update the Web site frequently and imaginatively that will make the difference.

The Webmaster

It is clear that design, development, and maintenance of a Web presence is a major corporate project that requires a significant budget and sound, continuous leadership to succeed. Thus, a corporate Webmaster is often critical to success.

The job description of a Webmaster is continuously being revised as the Web becomes an important function within a corporation. Whether a company decides to develop its Web site in-house or outsource it to a consulting organization, it still faces the issues of Web site reliability and accountability. Web site creation and maintenance is best delegated to a full-time Webmaster who has some idea about network administration, knows UNIX, and has a feel for aesthetics.

The best candidates for the Webmaster position are technically savvy specialists with one to two years of Web experience. The rapid development of Web technologies, however, may quickly outdate a person's capabilities faster than in other fields. Topics such as HTML 3, VRML, and Java are now the latest Web experience denominators, although those features are not yet supported by many Web design and navigation tools.

Aside from awareness of the latest technological trends in Web-associated technologies, the Webmaster must visualize how to design a Web site and implement the concept as an actual project. This implies a thorough understanding of the Web culture as a new business communications medium.

A successful Web site requires close attention on a 24-hour basis if it is to be globally competitive. The Webmaster must make sure that the Web site performs reliably, with minimal HTML errors, no invalid or dead-end links, and no Web server downtime.

In addition to smooth operations, the Webmaster must have a user monitoring program, taking care of all the feedback, bug reports, chat groups, and other issues that may arise from intensive user interaction with the corporate Web site.

Establishment and operation of a professional Web site is a time-consuming and labor-intensive undertaking that cannot be handled by a single Webmaster. At least two leaders are recommended to address the technical aspects of operating the Web servers and the design and maintenance of content. The technical Webmaster usually handles the system administration and maintenance, while the content Webmaster is responsible for the design, delivery, and updating of the information on the Web. Commercial-quality Web sites require full-time managers to handle both aspects of a Web operation.

Once the Web is established, the key to success is maintaining interesting new content. Continuously updating corporate press announcements, customer testimonials, and new links to other Web sites with additional information enhancing corporate products and services is critical to keep users returning on a regular basis.

Conclusions

The creation of a multimedia presence on the Web presents a considerable challenge to a corporation which must be prepared to design, develop, and maintain home pages on a 24-hour basis to present an effective and competitive worldwide presence on the Web.

The home page must identify the corporation, describe its mission, products and services, and provide links to related pages with detailed background information, images, and other multimedia features.

A good home page interface design is critical to success and should take into account the content of the page, clarity and simplicity of expression, use of color, graphics, audio, and video elements.

The complexity of a Web site and the variety of linkages between pages calls for advanced and careful planning with the support of top management. Storyboarding of the Web site is the best approach, resulting in a flow chart of the site and facilitating logical development of the project.

Web pages are developed using HTML language and a company must either acquire the skills to use it or contract with a specialized service to develop its Web site and pages. The HTML concept is based on placement of mark-up tags within text to define various elements of a page.

The introduction of images, audio and video into a Web site requires anchors associated with URL addresses of files which contain such multimedia content. Whether or not a user can receive multimedia content depends on the configuration of his or her Web browser and multimedia capabilities of the PC platform in use.

Once a Web site is developed, it must be placed on a Web server where 24-hour service and operation can be guaranteed. The Web site must also be announced to the Internet community to develop interest among users to visit it. One of the most effective ways of attracting users is to announce the new Web site and list it in various Web directories available on the Internet.

The design, development, and maintenance of a Web presence is a major corporate undertaking. It should receive top management support, a sufficient budget, and a full-time Webmaster to assure its success.

Chapter 8

World Wide Web Design and Manipulation Tools

There are Web design and manipulation tools available for several levels of user sophistication and new products are being developed every day. The basis for development of all Web tools is the Internet Engineering Task Force (IETF) and the Web Consortium which develop and define the standards for the HTML language.

These HTML level standards apply equally to the Web browser developers and all other design and manipulation tools at play in development and production of Web pages, sites, and servers. Some of those tools are Web page editors, HTML converters, and Web page integration suites that contain several interworking tools. The most sophisticated of those include Web browsers, the latest security features, and multimedia authoring tools.

Regardless of the Web design and manipulation tools, the developer must remember HTML level standards are in constant flux and that at no time will all potential users be able to access and download all of the contents of a Web page developed with a particular set of tools.

This is one of the main reasons why maintenance of the Web site is critical. If corporate home pages are to present a competitive image, they should contain the best multimedia elements that can be incorporated with the latest site development tools. Not everyone will be able to access all the multimedia elements on that Web site, but if intriguing icons and thumbnail images or videos are included at anchor points, this will keep the interest of the users. Users may even want to equip themselves with better Web browsers or multimedia viewers and return to a Web site that has caught their attention.

Hypertext Transport Protocol

Hypertext links are created using specific anchor tags of the HTML language, but when the user clicks on such an active link, a specific URL or the Web address of the object or file to which the link refers is designated.

The URL is called "universal" because it provides all the necessary information required by a Web browser about an object or a file to request, locate, and display it. In essence, the URL defines the protocol that should be followed to retrieve the document, the name of the computer or server on which it exists, and the path and filename of the document itself.

The *http://* part of a URL is the protocol indicator that shows the browser that the document exists on a Web server and indicates what rules must be followed to retrieve it. HTML pages almost always use the HTTP protocol, although some Web browsers can also retrieve documents from FTP, Gopher, Telnet, and Net News Transfer Protocol (NNTP).

The HTTP protocol is not a Web design and manipulation tool, but it is at the root of the HTML language and its inclusion in the URL must be regarded as an important element in the hyperlinking process.

The next part of the URL is the name of the remote Web server computer where a particular home page resides. More often than not, this server name starts with *www* to designate its presence on the Web, but this is not a mandatory designator and could be anything else. It has become an unwritten convention to indicate a computer dedicated as a Web server. This is followed by a specific network name of which the server forms a part with an extension such as *.com* or *.edu* indicating it is a commercial or educational organization.

The remaining part of the URL denotes the path and a filename of the Web document on the Web server. The file name often has an *.html* extension indicating an HTML file. This designator does not, however, indicate which HTML version or level with which the file complies.

Many URLs do not include a path or file name because Web servers automatically default to INDEX.HTML when specific file names are omitted. Often, organizations name their home pages *index.html* and locate them in root directories. As a result, many home pages of businesses can be guessed using corporate acronyms such as *att* or *ibm,* which will connect the user directly with the Web site of that company. A good Web design practice is to use a combination of subdirectories related to each other and the *index.html* default page.

HTML Editors

There are two types of editors on the market that facilitate the process of creating Web pages targeted at different categories of developers. These include graphical HTML editors and HTML tag editors. Many developers prefer to work with a Web page editor, which does not require manipulation of HTML tags because it is easier, faster, less expensive, and automatically insert the necessary tags when and where needed.

The graphical Web editor is an authoring tool that edits only the content of an HTML document. The use of such an editor precludes seeing any HTML tags and allows the developer to focus on content, images, graphics, and linkages. These tools offer an environment in which both the text and formatting can be inserted correctly and completely, and some offer syntax checking and correction. Several packages claim to be WYSIWYG tools, the image of a document will not necessarily be the same with all Web browsers. Table 8.1 presents a list of major HTML editors available on the Internet.

Table 8.1 Major HTML Editors

Product Name	Description and URL Address
ANT and ANT PLUS	This is a document template editor similar to Internet Assistant, but without browser mode; available for Windows and Macintosh at ftp://ftp.einet.net/einet/pc/ANT*
Emacs Helper Modes	HTML editing in WYSIWYG environment on UNIX platforms with Web browser options at http://www.santafe.edu/~nelson/tools/
FrontPage	Editor includes automated macro programs for creating pages and dropping Web objects http://www.vermeer.com

Product Name	Description and URL Address
Internet Assistant	Microsoft Windows-based editor with browser capability attached to Word http://www.microsoft.com/page/deskapp/word/ia/default.html
Live Markup	A standalone HTML editor for Windows platforms renders HTML elements similarly to how they appear in Web browsers http://www.mediatec.com/mediatech/
NaviPress 1.1	Editing Windows with identical HTML display to that of Netscape allows direct insertion of GIF and JPEG graphics http://www.navisoft.com
Nick Williams' Editor	Available for X-Windows platforms http://web.cs.city.ac.uk/homes/njw/htmltext/htmltxt.html
PageMill 1.0	http://www.adobe.com
Web Author	Word add-in HTML editor from Quarterdeck automatically converts Word documents to HTML files when saved http:/www.qdeck.com/

These graphical editing tools are available for all platforms including UNIX, Windows, Windows NT, and Macintosh. Many products are available in the form of freeware or shareware versions directly downloadable from the Internet, while professional versions can be obtained from vendors for a price. When selecting such tools, commercial products are probably maintained by their vendors and are likely to comply with the latest HTML versions. This feature alone makes it worth while to pay the price because there is no guarantee the free versions of such tools are updated in a timely manner. Many word processor programs provide HTML editors for use with their word processors, which then become graphical HTML authoring tools.

In the competitive environment of commercial Web servers, it is imperative to rapidly develop and update Web pages without using the latest HTML language version or HTTP protocols. While those pages can be developed readily with skilled HTML programmers, it is often more time and cost-effective to use a graphical Web page editor.

The main problem with Web authoring and editing tools is their overabundance. Large and small companies, and even individuals, develop specific editors and make them available on the Internet in the hopes of making a mark in cyberspace. Anyone using such tools will discover other programs require the user to fill in any features not included in a particular tool. In many cases, the final editing may have to be completed with an HTML tag editor to guarantee precise results when the Web page is accessed with several popular browsers.

Microsoft Internet Assistant

Microsoft Internet Assistant is a Web page editing package designed to convert the Word for Windows into a Web browser. The Internet Assistant operates in a an edit and browser mode. It is an excellent example of a graphical HTML editor associated with one of the most popular word processing packages.

In the edit mode, the Internet Assistant provides a Word toolbar with buttons for elements commonly required to create and edit HTML pages. No additional skills are required to create original HTML pages if the user knows how to handle the Word system. The Internet Assistant provides all the features of the Word word processor package.

The linkages with multimedia elements contained in external files are easily created by clicking the appropriate button on the Internet Assistant toolbar and entering the desired URL in a dialog box. The program is designed to instantly display an image at the point-of-choice in the HTML document, with an underlined shaded text that resembles an anchor in a browser. Clicking on such an anchor puts the user in the browser mode, while another click will test the linkage to other Web sites.

The Internet Assistant does not store original documents as HTML files. To create the final Web pages, it is necessary to save it as an HTML file on the Web server. This results in a certain amount of inconvenience when changing and updating such Web pages. Microsoft also provides a Word Viewer which allows users to see the HTML files without the need for Word, but a Windows operating environment is still required.

HTML Converter Tools or Filters

These are special programs that convert documents from one format to another, and are useful when the documents already exist in digital form. Also known as filters, these tools translate any existing document format into HTML without developing any HTML skills. No matter what word processor was used to create the original document, it is possible to save it in the rich text format (RTF) from which a number of converters can translate it rapidly into HTML pages.

The problem is the rapid proliferation of HTML converters as computer programmers continue to develop their own converters and post them on the Internet. Converters are also readily available for popular word processing packages in the Windows, Macintosh, and UNIX environments.

The W3 organization maintains an official list of HTML converters and filters on a Web site specifically designed for this purpose. It can be reached at:

http://www.w3.org/hypertext/WWW/tools/filters.html

There are also templates which are sets of formatting instructions that can be entered into a familiar editor. A document created using a template is saved directly as an HTML page, and is used to create new documents without learning new tools. On the other hand, templates often require the user to become familiar with HTML tags and their usage.

HTML Tag Editors

In contrast, an HTML tag editor assists the developer in creating required HTML tags. The tag elements are selected from menus or toolbars and the software creates a tag together with a closing tag. When attributes are needed to further refine the HTML page, a dialog box prompts the user to fill in the parameters and then provides the tags. Most HTML tag editors are specialized standalone packages not attached to other content generating software.

HoTMetal

HoTMetal is among the most popular HTML tag editors. It has been developed by SoftQuad of Toronto, Canada, but the system is menu-driven without the more common tool bar icons arrangement of popular contemporary tools. Some developers find it tiresome because it requires the continuous use of menus and insertion of HTML tags into the text. An enhanced version of this editor – HoTMetal Pro – is now available. It includes spell and syntax checking, macro creation, and a capability to insert next generation tags for tables.

HoTMetal is available at the NCSA Web site. Because the tool is so popular, however, this source is often very busy and alternative sources are suggested.

For example, it is also available at the **http://sq.com** site and the Web FAQ provides a list of other sites where HoTMetal can be found.

WebEdit

WebEdit is one of the newer HTML tag editors not associated with any word processors. It has been designed specifically with the HTML tag developer in mind, and can handle several HTML documents simultaneously in a multitasking system environment. WebEdit is also reportedly one of the most compliant with the very latest HTML 3 specifications, and provides the toolbar icon selection feature. WebEdit provides most commonly used tags for direct insertion into HTML pages speeding up the coding process for the developer. It is available at:

http://wwwnt.the group.net/Webedit/Webedit.html

Who Needs FTP?

The FTP is a well-established Internet tool used for retrieving and transferring files on Internet computers not on the Web. Web browsers and other HTML tools cannot be used to put such files on remote computers, but Web browsers can be used to retrieve and view such files. A Web browser can list a FTP server directory and any entry or it can be checked to download that particular file. However, not all Web browsers can handle FTP connectivity, although most of the advanced products are equipped with this facility.

The FTP is a resource tool because many computers not on the Web contain useful information, including multimedia content that may be proprietary to a business. In fact, some of these computers may also include files in HTML format that could be used directly on the Web without needing to be edited.

Access to FTP computers is controlled through URLs, which may have a *ftp://* protocol indicator at the beginning. The addresses of these files vary, however, depending on whether they are anonymous or non-anonymous FTP computer systems.

Anonymous FTP provides connectivity to any computer on the Internet with an FTP server, regardless of whether the user has an account and password for that particular computer. When anonymous FTP computers are accessed with a Web browser, the details of making the connection and logging-in are managed by the browser. Once the FTP file is retrieved, it can be saved by the user for further manipulation with appropriate tools.

Non-anonymous FTP access differs from anonymous FTP because it requires end-user account and password for log-in to a remote computer. The URLs for non-anonymous FTP connectivity must include the user's name and password in the address. Once the proper account name and password are recognized, the system provides lists of files in the home directories similar to the way an anonymous FTP handles directories. Specific files and subdirectories can be selected and downloaded as necessary.

When such resources are available through a Web home page with a non-anonymous FTP connection, the user name and password are also available for all to see. It is, therefore, absolutely necessary to design Web pages with FTP sources so account numbers and used in retrieval of materials are not transferred to the public Web pages.

Most Web browsers support the FTP protocol and a FTP site at NCSA can be reached for more information on the FTP protocol at:

ftp://ftp.ncsa.uiuc.edu/Web/Mosaic/windows

How Useful Is Gopher?

Gopher is another Internet protocol and resource designed to make Internet access easy for the masses before the development of the Web. It is a global menu-based selection system displaying lists of options. Users can make a selection clicking on a particular entry on a list, which brings up another menu with lower level options or a final document page. It is similar to the HTML concept where many choices link the user with other menus or documents resident on computers throughout the world.

Although the Gopher system is comprehensive and many of its documents may present significant value, it is relatively simple when compared with the Web. The Gopher system is strictly text-based and does not provide the basic graphics for headings, fonts or sizes. Nevertheless, because of its simplicity, it is easy to include Gopher capability in Web browsers. Gopher servers exist on many computers worldwide, mostly at universities and their URLs are identified by *gopher://* in the first part of the address.

Creating a link to a Gopher resource from a Web page is simple and done in a manner similar to creating anchors and links to other Web servers. Gopher links will only produce text files. Because these are non-graphic textual pages, they will not appear to be part of a professional Web presentation or marketing site unless considerable work is done on them with HTML editors.

Imagemapping of Web Pages

One of graphics and multimedia practices on the Web home pages is the inclusion of imagemaps. These are collections of logos, graphics or names arranged in an elegant and highly colorful manner at the top of a Web page. An imagemap can contain a graphical "hot spot" linkage under each image and users can click on those images to obtain more information about the products or services represented by those images.

A relatively simple imagemap can greatly enhance a Web page. Some of the cybermall pages are excellent examples of imagemaps in practice. In those cases, the entire Web page is designed to represent various storefronts available at the cybermall with merchant names, graphics, and logos indicative of the types of products handled by individual vendors. Clicking on these items usually brings the user into the specific store which is more often than not another imagemap of product displays and service offerings.

Development of an imagemap is a relatively complex and tedious effort and involves creating and locating useful images, selecting and assigning specific areas to be linkage hot-spots, and integrating the complete imagemap subsystem into the Web server.

Creating proprietary images for use in imagemaps is now generally preferred. Although there are thousands of images available on the Web, most are not available with proprietary customizable qualities. Such images can now be easily created with graphics programs and saved as GIF files, readily supported by most browsers.

Once the GIF files are available, there are several free or commercial packages that can be used to map the images. Developers can choose from several of the most popular Web server formats to create the proper map file for a particular server.

It is then necessary to create a link in the HTML page that refers to the imagemap program, indicates the location of the imagemap file, and identifies file path to the GIF image to be displayed. These are still not the simplest procedures, but new Web development tools are being developed to simplify the process even further.

This type of multimedia Web content is going to become more common as competition intensifies. The best advice for developers who want to create imagemap Web pages quickly is to hire experts who have experience developing imagemaps. This is particularly true if the Web site is to be resident on a UNIX Web server for which available tools are more complex.

Imagemap Editor Tools

The WebSite Imagemap Editor is a commercial imagemap tool from O'Reilly & Associates. It is a relatively simple tool that requires marking the hot spots on an open GIF image and assigning URLs and descriptive comments to each. The program includes URLs which display the imagemap to the user.

MapTHIS is another imagemap tool program for Windows available free of charge. It provides a toolbar with rectangles, circles, ovals or polygons for defining hot spots on the image which can be stretched to cover the sensitive area on the image. Other imagemapping programs available for Windows, Macintosh, and UNIX environments. Table 8.2 presents a list of several imagemapping tools available for use on the Internet with their URL addresses.

Table 8.2 Selected Imagemapping Tools

Product Name	Description and URL Address
glorglox	Image mapping tool for UNIX environments http://www.uunet.ca/~tomr/glorglox/
MapTHIS!	Image mapping tool for Windows platform http://galadriel.ecaetc.ohio-state.edu/tc/mt
Mapedit	A tool for Windows and X-Windows http://sunsite.unc.edu/boutell/mapedit/mapedit.html
MapMaker	Tool for X-Windows http://icg.stwing.upenn.edu/~mengwong/mapmaker.html
WebMac	Image mapping tool for Macintosh http://arppl.carleton.ca/machttp/doc/util/map/webmap.html
WebSite Image Map Editor	Part of WebSite Windows NT server http://www.ora.com

Multimedia Authoring on the Web

Initial tools for integrating multimedia into documents published on the Web are now appearing on the market. Macromedia, a leading multimedia authoring tool vendor, introduced the Shockwave playback technology for its Director multimedia authoring system. Shockwave allows users to view multimedia content created with the Director authoring tool within the Internet browser application or the Web home page. Shockwave is a free software product which is being incorporated into the Netscape Navigator 2.0 Web browser.

The Java Scene

The Java programming language developed by Sun Microsystems can be used by Web developers to animate HTML pages. It is targeted at Web page design editors and seasoned C++ programmers. Java is similar to C and C++ and is an object-oriented, flexible, and extensible language with capabilities beyond HTML-based interactivity. Java enables users to create applets such as animations or real-time stock tickers that enhance static HTML pages.

The Java engine is a combination of the C and C++ languages optimized for online C/S applications. Java applets serve as carriers for the code which can be configured to perform a number of applications. The Java language is multithreaded, therefore, each applet can perform multiple tasks and link other applets for continuous animation.

On the other hand, Java lacks tools for non-programmers. Higher level tools are needed to promote wide use of Java and incorporation of the technology into Web design and manipulation tools. It is also an element of more creative tools such as the Java Animation Machine (JAM), which is a 2-D animation package for developing Java applets without major programming.

Sun Microsystems and Netscape are attempting to alleviate this situation with their joint development of JavaScript. This product is a cross-platform, object-oriented scripting language for designing active Web pages with audio and animated interactive elements. It can animate elements of HTML Web pages which will respond to a Java-enabled browser. JavaScript is an easier development environment, which is distributed free of charge by Sun and Netscape.

Java is an interpretive language that allows programs to be compiled "on-the-fly," and is platform independent. A Java application is written once and it will run on any platform where a Java interpreter resides. This allows Webmasters to update Web applications across the Internet at run time. Java interpreters also exist in Web browsers including Sun's HotJava, Netscape's Navigator 2.0, and the latest Spyglass Mosaic. Sun is developing Java support on Windows NT, Windows 95, Macintosh, Solaris, and other operating systems.

Java allows the Web browser to be the full-featured, application development platform competing with the functions underlying operating systems. The major concern about Java is that its applets might open undetectable security holes on a user computer. Nevertheless, a number of tool vendors are supporting Java including multimedia authoring software developers such as Macromedia, which includes Java in the Authorware and Director authoring systems.

The Blackbird to Internet Studio Saga

Microsoft is developing the Blackbird and MediaView tools for its Microsoft Network (MSN) online service. The company is now competing with vendors that create Web navigation and site development tools because many content providers want to take advantage of the Web.

Blackbird is a multimedia authoring tool that provides a better way to design graphic logos and icons. It is based on Visual Basic OLE technology and provides a viewer/development environment originally designed for MSN and HTTP servers. Now that Microsoft repositioned the MSN as an Internet access system, it has renamed Blackbird as Internet Studio to compete with Java as an alternative Web page authoring tool.

Blackbird was conceived as a competitive software tool to Java and a Web version is now in beta stages. The authoring tool can handle multimedia extensions to a Web page such as background music, manipulable 3-D objects, and inline video in Microsoft AVI file format. The product supports OLE and OLE controls technology – OLE commands (OCX) – and is now operating with MSN, but it is being modified to work with the Web.

Microsoft is pursuing a two-pronged strategy, trying to leverage a large number of Visual Basic programmers and capture a significant market share of

Java aficionados. The Internet Studio, based on Visual Basic, remains the primary marketing focus in Microsoft's Web strategy. Users of this system have the advantage of not having to learn a new language.

The Promise of Virtual Reality Modeling Language

VRML is the next generation software development tool that allows the addition of 3-D environments to Web graphics and multimedia. It departs from the standard HTML based on text. VRML relies on creating an environment for intuitive interaction rather than the use of textual menus. This new technology is expected to become the cornerstone of future electronic commerce applications and will allow users to develop their own 3-D Web sites.

VRML is gaining rapid acceptance because it allows users to build VRML worlds on the Web from 3-D scenes created by standard graphics packages. In addition, VRML files can be created and viewed on several platforms including Windows 3.1, Windows 95, Macintosh, and UNIX. From the point of view of massive data transmission and compression, VRML is much easier to display online than real-time video because it requires fewer bits to construct polygons than massive megabytes for storing and displaying video.

Current VRML is not yet able to communicate with multiple users. Future versions of VRML are expected to provide higher levels of control and cyberspace interactivity, while VRML 2.0 specification calls for multiuser interaction. More details of initial VRML products are available at: http://intervista.com. A beta version of the WorldView VRML module also can be downloaded that allows viewing and navigating VRML Web sites. Fountain software from Caligari Corporation is a VRML version of its TrueSpace 3-D authoring tool, which lets users create and view VRML worlds on the Web. It is available at: http://caligari.com. To truly appreciate the VRML products, users require very fast Pentium processors and 3-D accelerators.

Microsoft announced V-Chat communications tool based on VRML technology which supports 2-D and 3-D environments. Users can represent themselves as online icons – avatars – and control their animated gestures and movements using a toolbar at the client program.

Worlds, Inc., a software developer, already offers an extension to the VRML known as VRML+. This is a specialized tool for creating interactive 3-D landscapes in which online customers can develop communication with other users and purchase goods in virtual stores using credit cards secured by encryption methods. There is some interest in using VRML+ to develop virtual trade shows with 3-D booths, its usage is limited by the requirement for high-bandwidth connections to communicate with such 3-D virtual cybermalls. Although VRML+ can work with a 14.4Kbps modem, the response times in some areas could be a problem when extensive graphics must be transmitted interactively to users. VRML+ allows the creation of various interactive agents that appear on the screens as virtual tellers in banks or clerks in stores with whom users can communicate. VRML+ is an open specification and it is available from Worlds Web site at **http://www.worlds.net**.

IBM recently announced a VRML+ server and browser software that supports the new language, while Visa International has designed its Electronic Courtyard based on this language. It is a Web site within which banks and retail shops can set-up their branches and storefronts. The IBM VRML+ software runs on RISC System/6000 and is expected to be ported later to Windows NT and Solaris platforms. The original VRML runs only on powerful SGI workstations.

Conclusions

Web page design and manipulation tools depend on HTML language standards which apply equally to Web servers, browsers and other editing tools. Because HTML standards are in constant development, special care must be taken in selecting the proper Web site design tools to make sure that the largest possible number of users will be able to access the site.

The HTML editors come in two distinct categories and facilitate the process of creating Web pages. The graphical HTML editors handle only the content of an HTML document while HTML tag editors assist in creating the HTML tags and attributes within the text.

There are also HTML converter tools or filters for translating existing document formats to HTML without the need for HTML programming skills. There is also an overabundance of such tools on the Internet because many programmers create their own products and post them on the Internet in expectation of developing business for themselves.

Several major Web page editing packages have gained prominence as popular design tools. These include Internet Assistant, HoTMetal, WebEdit, and others.

The other Internet protocols including FTP and Gopher are also worth considering as sources of HTML and other documents suitable for referencing them from the Web home pages.

For graphics and multimedia content, imagemapping tools are valuable in enhancing Web pages. This type of Web page development was relatively complex previously but imagemapping tools have simplified and popularized their use. Nevertheless, creation of multimedia images and content for inclusion on Web pages remains a complex and separate issue.

Chapter 9

World Wide Web Development Services

Companies developing Web sites and servers for LAN and WAN connectivity throughout the enterprise face sophisticated search engines, complex security systems, and an array of unfamiliar Web design and development software products. Usually, they do not possess in-house capabilities for undertaking such projects without a costly and lengthy learning process. In cases where competitive pressures mandate faster development of a Web presence, the best alternative is to outsource such work from a flexible and reliable consulting organization.

This is easier said than done because Web design and development technology is so new. Web-related software products are often not standardized, and new versions are released literally every few weeks if not more often.

There are a number of service firms that provide various levels of Web development assistance. These include Internet access providers, Web page designers, HTML programmers, Web security specialists, Web server developers, Web site maintenance suppliers, and Web performance analysts.

Different companies offer varying levels of skills and different combinations of services.

Long-distance and regional Bell operating companies (RBOCs) are a special group of service companies offering Web services associated with Internet access capabilities and Internet backbone facilities. The strengths of telephone carrier companies lies in their unmatched experience building high-speed data networks for transmitting multimedia files and content. They also have an edge in existing large corporate user accounts, which they can convert into Web service accounts at competitive rates.

Leading systems integrators are positioning themselves to become major players as Web site creation and hosting services providers. There also are many Web service providers, ranging from small groups of HTML programmers to turnkey Web server design and implementation services offered by the "Big 6" and other IT consulting organizations.

If Web site operators are planning to engage in electronic commerce, they will require highly interactive Web pages where users can complete electronic forms and transmit personal information and credit card data through secure channels. Such designs will require custom programming probably at the HTML level, which is not an easy task. Some ISPs provide such services to their Web access clients, but if there is a significant amount of maintenance and updating involved, the company may want to set-up its own in-house Web server design and operation.

Unless an in-house capability is established, the only alternative is to depend on outside consultants. The first step is to select an appropriate consulting organization to perform the task in a cost-effective manner. This in itself is difficult to achieve until the purpose and scope of the proposed Web presence program is identified.

Where the Markets Are

There are several market segments related to Web development and maintenance services. These include Internet access, security consultation and implementation, Web server design and management, electronic commerce software, interactive advertising, and Web site performance evaluation and analysis. There are also associated markets dealing with integration of Web presence and associated environments with existing corporate networks, servers, databases, and archives.

Of those market segments, selling Internet access is the most concrete business at present. The reason is that most corporate clients are primarily testing the Web and its capabilities, trying to determine a strategic potential for their businesses.

To test the Web potential companies must gain access to it and establish connectivity suitable to transmit multimedia content at some acceptable data rate. Therefore, according to The Yankee Group, Internet access revenues were estimated at about $400 million in 1995, but are expected to increase rapidly to approximately $1.8 billion as soon as 1998. Figure 9.1 illustrates this growth.

Figure 9.1 Internet Access Revenues

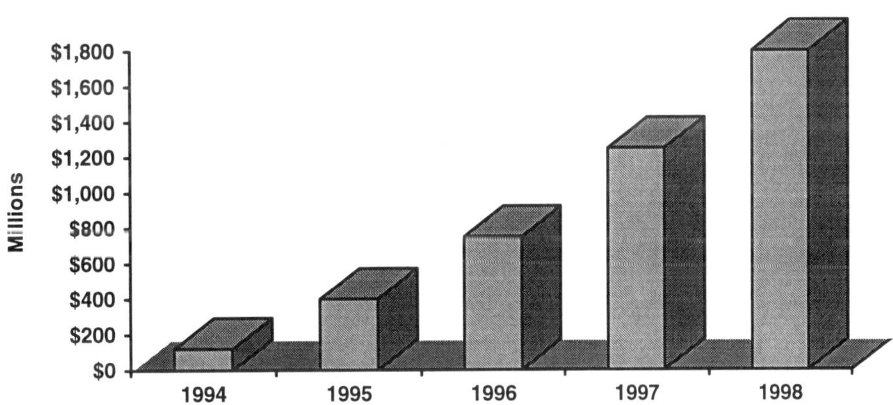

Source: The Yankee Group

Web Server Market Forecasts

The Web server market consists of revenues received by Internet service providers, computer companies, and IT consultants that assist corporations in doing business on the Web. Forrester Research of Cambridge, Massachusetts, completed a study of the Web business market which estimated the 1995 Web server market at a minuscule $5 million, although it is expected to increase to more than $600 million by the year 2000.

The study recognizes three segments of the Web server market. These include companies assisting others to create a Web presence in form of a home page, software vendors creating tools for developing home pages, and firms that can assist Web marketers in doing business on the Web. One factor that keeps this market segment from growing faster is the fact that many companies do not know what they want to sell on the Internet. Trying to sell their traditional products electronically does not necessarily guarantee success and there is a dearth of experience of what products sell online and why. Customized versions of existing products are believed to be the most likely to succeed in this market segment.

Who Has the Most Points of Presence?

While IPSs are the most obvious sources of Web server and site development assistance – and there are hundreds if not thousands of such firms all over the world – IPSs are considered to be only significant regional and national operators. From the Web site sponsor's perspective, the number of points of presence that these vendors offer is important because it indicates their coverage in a country or the world. In this respect, it is becoming clear that the telecommunications companies are going to be the clear winners in the long run because of their existing transmission facilities and various levels of services, many of which are being upgraded to handle multimedia traffic at competitive rates.

Given the need to establish multimedia access to the Web site for users worldwide, it is important to make sure that the facilities offered by the chosen ISP are adequate to handle such traffic without undue delays and bottlenecks.

Multimedia Services Affiliate Forum

An interesting development with regard to Web presence and operation is the initiative that developed at the latest Telecom 95 conference in Switzerland. It is a proposal involving several telephone carriers to develop a global multimedia network to facilitate the transmission of multimedia traffic throughout the world.

The objective of the Multimedia Services Affiliate Forum (MSAF) is to provide a public and secure multimedia network that will conform to common interoperability standards and act as a multimedia data highway. It would support applications such as videoconferencing and collaborative computing, and the trials for this service are expected to begin during 1996. MSAF is supported by AT&T, Deutsche Telekom, NTT, Telecom Netherlands, Telia, Swiss Telecom, Telefonica SA and major software vendors including Lotus, Novell, and Intel ProShare.

Tracking World Wide Web Demographics

Companies with Web sites are increasingly interested in tracking the number and demographics of the visitors to their site. Web site tracking tools are becoming important as companies try to evaluate and interpret visits to their Web servers. Several new ventures with specialized software to perform such tasks are now coming to market.

Demographics are critical for good Web management and are of immediate interest to Webmasters in any company that maintains a presence on the Web. They are also invaluable to advertising agencies that are becoming involved with interactive online advertising. Analysis of traffic patterns around a Web site enable Webmasters to reorganize Web pages to make them most appealing and easy-to-use by all visitors.

Logical Design Solutions, Inc., of Murray Hill, New Jersey, developed WebTrac software that analyzes data from Web servers running on major platforms such as Windows, Macintosh or UNIX. WebTrac is specifically designed for companies that have established a Web server and are interested in monitoring the traffic at their site. WebTrac does not include registration of Web visitors because early attempts to do so met with user resistance. Nevertheless, this is considered a major issue by companies that plan to track Web traffic internally.

WebTrac software resides on the server and it reads time, geographical location, and other data available from the browsers used by those who access the Web server. Data is transmitted directly to the desktop under Windows using Microsoft FoxPro. Once downloaded to a PC, WebTrac provides design tools for translating the data into region maps, line graphs, bar, and pie charts as required. WebTrac is priced at $5,000.

Internet Profile Corporation (I/Pro) of San Francisco is another new venture involved in measuring the performance of the Web traffic. Its software accumulates hits on a Web site through an internal program that tags visitors and collects their IP addresses. Special proprietary algorithms are then used to estimate actual traffic rates.

I/Pro is a new venture less than two years old but because of its critical activity in interactive communications it caught the attention of Nielsen Media Research which provides weekly TV ratings for the advertising industry. Nielsen, a subsidiary of Dun & Bradstreet, bought an unspecified stake in I/Pro and plans to collaborate in increasing the measurement criteria of the Web auditing system and enhance the reports for easier interpretation. The objective is to provide weekly Web popularity ratings comparable to TV ratings.

A similar product was developed by Digital Planet Corporation known as NetCount. These ventures announced recently that as a service to Madison Avenue executives they intend to rate Web home pages and rank the most popular hyperlinks. The advertising industry is intrigued by the concept of interactive advertising and is eager to acquire pertinent demographic data about it. Other forms of tracking Web demographics are performed by WebTrak of New York, which is initiating a Web rating service by ranking Web sites by the number of times they appear on browser lists.

The Rush toward Web Consulting Services

Most ISPs are well aware by now that access to the Internet will eventually become a commodity probably supplied in a most competitive manner by the major carriers. After all, these large companies are the providers of the backbones and switching facilities that make the Internet and Web traffic a reality. Except for a few larger independent organizations, most Internet access providers lease or rent transmission capacity from the major carriers and even from each other and become local or regional resellers. This will continue until the market stabilizes and the major carriers start offering high-speed facilities to all Internet users at such competitive prices that most ISPs in reseller status will not be able to compete.

Leading ISPs were initially hoping to make a name for themselves in those early days by providing access to the Internet, but now they want to become the suppliers of more sophisticated Web services. These services include Web server design, home page programming, firewall construction, data encryption or cybermall marketing projects.

Every smaller company in the Web service business is trying to position itself to become a consulting organization, showing large corporate clients how to exploit the Web to its best strategic advantage. To do this, these ventures are acquiring the knowledge and skills required to establish Web connectivity, run initial tests, develop home pages, put together a Web site, and migrate clients to a Web server that they may maintain and update on a regular basis. It is clear that a whole new type of services is emerging, which will operate "farms" of Web servers each specializing in a different stage of corporate Web presence development or dedicated to a particular corporate client on a permanent basis.

To achieve this status, most vendors must first become consulting organizations and they are moving toward that goal from several directions. ISPs are only one type of venture with the advantage of a clientele for which initial Web access is arranged. Web tools developers, companies producing Web browsers and home page editors, also are looking forward to that same market. Their policy is to give away the relatively basic Web browsing of editing software to establish large client bases. These clients can then be offered more sophisticated Web development and maintenance products that must be supported by continuous consulting and training programs.

At present, the Web consulting market is estimated to average about $50,000 per client, providing initial connectivity and Web site development advice. It is expected to continue to grow for the rest of this century until most corporations establish Web servers and operations or decide after initial testing that there is no profit for them in such activities.

The Web presence starter kit market is clearly one with limited scope and will be affected by development of other interactive services targeting the consumer such as interactive TV or special online services developed by cable TV and telephone carriers. All these alternatives, once they have the facilities to provide low-cost Web access to large numbers of consumers, will eliminate the need for Web starter kit services. However, these services may also create new opportunities for publishers, advertisers, and promoters by simply providing new means for distributing existing skills and services.

AT&T WorldNet Managed Internet Service

The long-distance carrier announced its AT&T WorldNet service in late 1995. This service is designed to enable businesses to access, plan, operate, manage, and maintain leased access to the Internet using AT&T facilities.

In addition, customers receive expert Web presence implementation support and active monitoring of service levels with problem diagnosis and resolution. AT&T is providing this comprehensive service in conjunction with BBN Planet, which is an ISP in its own right with extensive networking consulting capabilities and expertise.

AT&T Hosting and Transaction Services is targeted at the 800 toll-free number businesses that would like to extend their marketing efforts into the Web environment. AT&T will set-up Web sites linked to databases for processing transactions for its merchants and helping promote and sell products on the Internet.

AT&T Content Services Interchange Online Network collaborates with content providers and developers. It provides specialized networking infrastructures and linkages to the Internet for information and entertainment services to consumers, businesses, and professionals.

More details about AT&T WorldNet services is available at (800) 309-3349 and at **http://www.att.com/worldnet**.

CommerceNet

CommerceNet, of Menlo Park, California is a consortium of more than 100 organizations and companies organized specifically to research and report on electronic commerce and associated issues. CommerceNet does not provide any Web services, but it has nine working groups investigating issues such as Internet security, directories, catalogs, payment systems connectivity, marketing, collaboration tools, public policy, and engineering data transfer.

CommerceNet published reports on what approaches work, which do not, and why. The organization also will propose that working strategies should become Web operating standards facilitating the development of electronic commerce on the Internet.

The organization's latest projects include development of Internet services that are affordable for small companies and exploration of how the technology can be exploited in the government procurement process.

EDS Interactive Multimedia Services

EDS, a leading systems integrator located in Plano, Texas, developed EDS Interactive Multimedia Services to provide Web site creation and content hosting capabilities as an extension to its Internet access services. In addition to its own services, EDS is willing to work with various access providers selected by its clients, and will provide Web site performance measurement and analysis. This is a valuable service to corporations that are planning to engage in electronic commerce on the Web. There is a requirement for experience and specialized tools to perform such analysis that are not necessarily known or readily available to newcomers to such online businesses. EDS also provides integration of connectivity and applications into customized online environments. More details about EDS Web services are available at (214) 605-5041.

Industry.Net

Industry.Net is one of the most successful Web services providing an online marketplace for manufacturing and industrial clients. Industry.Net maintains a Web site on which it offers businesses a facility to shop for industrial goods and products. The service provides electronic storefronts for manufacturers and suppliers who are charged from $3,000 to $8,000 annually to participate.

The service located in Pittsburgh, Pennsylvania, does not provide online transactions but businesses can place orders using electronic mail. In future the venture plans to also provide online purchasing to its clients.

More recently, Industry.Net launched an online catalog service which allows customers to shop for specific products within a manufacturer's Web site. Participation fees in the catalog are quite steep, however, ranging from $8,000 to $500,000 depending on the size of the Web site and contract duration.

Internet Shopping Network

This subsidiary of the Home Shopping Network provides a service for merchants who do not have the capabilities to develop their own Web servers. The "cybermall" is based on the Netscape Commerce server on which companies can rent shop fronts and put up home pages describing their products and services. Initial services include a catalogue of more than 22,000 computer products, 40,000 music titles in 21 genres, and specific merchants such as FTD Flowers, Omaha Steaks, and Hammacher-Schlemmer Gifts. The service offers data encryption and authentication for credit card transactions. More details are available at **http://shop.internet.net.**

MarketplaceMCI

This is among the largest of all cybermalls created by MCI in 1995, designed to offer secure Internet shopping environment. It is a specialized electronic commerce service targeting Fortune 1000 organizations offering development of electronic shop fronts at costs ranging from $25,000 to $100,000. Participation in the cybermall is rented at monthly fees ranging from $2,000 to $10,000, depending on size and location of the electronic storefront. The service provides toll-free 800 user access to the cybermall and electronic shopping baskets, which allow users to collect purchases from several merchants and pay only once with a credit card when the purchasing visit is complete. The service offers complete turnkey development and operation for corporate clients, but it is not inexpensive. There are transaction charges based on amount of business performed by a storefront in the cybermall. More details can be obtained at **http://www.internetMCI.com**.

Netcom Online Communications Services

Located in San Jose, California, Netcom is the leading independent Internet access provider, handling at least 200 points of presence throughout the world. Netcom provides dial-up access for individuals and dedicated communications lines to corporate clients.

Netcom built one the largest subscriber bases by selling to individuals and is seen as the lowest-cost service provider. Initial Web access account starts at $19.95 per month for 40 hours, but its facilities are mostly 14.4 Kbps and 28.8 Kbps modem lines which are not the best solution for Web interaction.

Performance Systems International

Performance Systems International (PSI) located in Herndon, Virginia, is a small firm considered to be a leading Internet access provider with revenues of $15.2 million in 1994. This venture provides Internet access services to not just large commercial customers, but also to individual dial-up clients. The company provides managed commercial Internet access for organizations, Web hosting services, and several internetworking services.

PSI recently acquired the Pipeline Network of New York, and the resulting venture now has more than 14,000 subscribers. The company had a $5.3 million loss in 1994, but this did not stop PSI from going public at $12 per share in a stock offering which turned out to be heavily oversubscribed. PSI plans to spend $10 million of the funds raised to double its points of presence to about 200.

UUNet Technologies

UUNet Technologies located in Fairfax, Virginia, is a major Internet access venture providing dial-up and dedicated commercial access for individuals, workgroups, and companies. It also provides Web hosting services and is expanding its capabilities to become a more complete consulting organization.

UUNet Technologies, which is an eight-year old venture, has grown rapidly from $1.36 million in revenues in 1990, to $12.41 million in 1994. Revenues were expected to reach $45 million or more in during 1995. This represents spectacular growth, but the company experienced equally significant losses during the last two years which reached almost $7 million in 1994. Nevertheless, UUNet Technologies is seen as a favorite in its market niche because of its special relationship with Microsoft. Under a special agreement, UUNet is providing exclusive Internet access to users of the new Microsoft Network. Microsoft acquired 15% of the equity of UUNet for about $15 million and is expected to provide approximately another $26 million in loans during the next five years to finance networking equipment purchases for the Microsoft Network.

UUNet also announced new products and services designed to provide security and confidentiality for corporate data as it traverses the Internet to business partners or remote sites. In addition, the company intends to design and maintain Internet-based security for companies interested in outsourcing such tasks. This is particularly valuable to corporations sending CAD and manufacturing data in collaborative environments where a very high level of data security is required. The product, known as LanGuardian, is a T-1 packet switch with built-in encryption designed to encrypt information sent between a defined source and destination on the Internet. The company also acts as an

OEM reseller for Gauntlet Firewall which controls Internet access to the corporate networks.

Web Service Providers Galore

There are literally thousands of Web service providers handling all the various aspects of Web site design and maintenance, with a number of larger organizations that provide full turnkey services.

It is impossible to list all of these organizations because they are literally emerging overnight. Table 9.1 represents a selection of some of the more prominent Web service providers in various categories. These include complete turnkey organizations, ISPs with Web hosting services, and consulting ventures specializing in design of Web pages, sites, servers at various levels. Some are specialists in design of the page layout and associated marketing and advertising content. Others provide basic HTML programming, but there are usually combinations of skills available from many small firms. It is the responsibility of a Webmaster to identify and evaluate such consulting organizations before undertaking a Web presence project for a corporation.

Table 9.1 Selected Web Service Providers

Service Name	Description and URL Address
AT&T WorldNet	Comprehensive turnkey Web services including Web access, implementation, and management offered in conjunction with BBN Planet as a consulting partner http://www.att.com/worldnet
BBN Planet	Major regional ISP offering Web hosting service, network security, monitoring, training, and consulting http://www.bbnplanet.com
BBS One Online Services	Assists in creating Web presence to business and other organizations http:\www.prgone.com
Bedrock Information Solutions	Provides Web page creation, HTML authoring, Internet services, and Internet development http://www.bedrock.com/
CompuServe	SPRYTE service provides home page Wizard which allows users to develop a Web page Tel: 206/442-2598
Computing Engineers	Provides Worldwide Access and MagicServer Web server presence development and consulting services http://www.wwa.com/
Computing Support Team	Provides Web page design, servicing, and consulting services http://www.gems.com/

Service Name	Description and URL Address
Databack Services	Web presence consulting and page design http://www.dbserv.com/dbs/
Digital Creators	Development of Web applications and software http://www.digicod.com
Duke-Net	Personal and business Web page design at very low cost; additional updating charges http://www.duke-net.com
EDS Interactive Multimedia Service	ISP with Web site creation; Web hosting performance analysis and system integration http://www.eds.com
Electric Press	Web publisher specializing in Web presence creation for companies; also provides dedicated Web servers http://www.elpress.com
Free Range Media	Web production and Internet services creating online environments and interactive Web promotions http://www.freerange.com
Home Pages	Designs and maintains Web pages for clients http://www.homepages.com
IBM	Web server hosting services; manages access, security, and full range of Internet hardware and software products http://www.infomkt.ibm.com
Ides Communications Group	Development and management of Web sites http://www.ides.com
InfoMatch Communications	Develops Web pages, HTML authoring, and other Internet services http://infomatch.com:70
Internet Media Group	Provides Web pages design, creation, advertising services, high-speed access, and consulting services http://www.mailorder.com
Laran Communications	Specializes in online classified advertising providing its services on the Web including instructions for placing ads http://www.webpads.com
Mainsail Marketing	Provides virtual catalogs for direct marketing and handles single Web pages or complete Web sites and servers for clients http://www.mainsail.com
Mainstream Netservice	Web server operation for business presentations in English or Dutch http://www.mainstream.nl
MCI	MarketplaceMCI is a Web server offering largest electronic cybermall service http://www.mci.com
NetGrafx	Specializes in creating Web pages for corporate Web presence http://www.netgrafx.com
One World Information Services	Provides marketing information for maximizing Web presence visibility http://oneworld.wa.com
Online Solutions	Develops Web pages for advertisers http://www.amsquare.com/america/online.html
PSINet	ISP company with Web hosting services and ISDN

Service Name	Description and URL Address
RS Communication	Provides Web development services including graphics, imaging, and networking http://www.rscomm.com
Teleport	Regional Web service includes HTML authoring and applications development http://www.teleport.com
UUNet Technologies	Major national ISP with Web hosting services; Microsoft has a stake in this company http://www.uu.com
Vanderlay Industries	Provides marketing design products and services for Web sites and servers http://www.vanderlay.com
WWW Service Providers	Web site provides a list of vendors that offer Web server design and development servers as well as HTML authoring and applications ftp://ftp.einet.net/pub/INET-MARKETING/www.suc-providers

Conclusions

There are major business opportunities in establishing a corporate Web presence, and a large number of ventures are positioning themselves to take advantage of this emerging market. Services that are likely to be in demand include Web page, site, and server design and development, construction of firewalls, encryption of commercial transactions, tracking of Web site traffic demographics, interactive advertising, and electronic commerce cybermalls.

For the corporation that needs to establish a Web presence, but does not possess the required skills or time to acquire such capabilities, there are numerous services that can assist in the process. Ultimate decisions on the use of outside assistance will be based on the experiences with initial Web site operation and applicability of Web marketing or presence to the corporate environment. Companies facing extensive Web server development and maintenance are probably better off in developing comprehensive in-house skills for this purpose.

Web development service providers range from large system integrators and Internet access providers who can offer turnkey solutions to small consulting ventures specializing in only one or two aspects of the business.

Internet and Web access is expected to become a commodity market in the next few years controlled by major telecommunications carriers. As a result many small and marginal ISPs are developing Web design and maintenance consulting skills which they perceive as the mainstay of their future business.

Chapter 10

Conclusions

The Web is expected to significantly change the way business is conducted around the world. Whether or not this happens, most business entities – large and small alike – are rushing to establish a presence on the Web.

What is now becoming clear, however, is that in many instances, a Web presence is not necessarily beneficial. In fact, some observers suggest that it is better not to even have a Web presence unless it is fully supported by corporate management, and designed and implemented with top-quality talent and resources.

Multimedia on the Web Makes the Difference

Since the introduction of the Web with multimedia content storage and transmission capabilities, the Internet has become an important new medium for business transactions. The Web is the fastest growing segment of the Internet as companies rush to establish their presence in form of Web servers or home pages promoting their products and services. Nevertheless, there are a number of issues that are still unresolved and must be taken into account when establishing a Web presence on the Internet.

Despite considerable progress in developing encryption software, firewalls, and secure transaction services which protect corporate networks from unauthorized access by undesirable Internet users, transaction security issues are not fully resolved and there is doubt that a perfect solution will ever exist.

Most communications links are inadequate for transmission of multimedia content from Web sites. This means special consideration must be given to the design of Web servers and sites with multimedia content.

Yet the Web is becoming the main source of multimedia content and activity on the Internet. This is accessible through the use of specially configured Web browsers and appropriate multimedia capable platforms operated by the user.

The Web Is a Complex Environment

The Web is a network of multimedia resources within the Internet which are distinct from other information resources, and are linked with each other using HTTP. Web servers and sites contain text, sound, graphics, and video files which can be located, retrieved, and viewed using Web client software such as browsers.

The key to Web operations is the URL or specific address of a document that makes it possible to access information throughout the Internet regardless of the operating platforms and communications protocols.

Successful use of the Web for multimedia traffic also depends on availability of adequate bandwidth in communication links between the Web servers and clients. Development of high-speed digital facilities inside and outside corporate environments is accelerating the availability of multimedia transmission services and increasing the business potential of the Web.

Yes, There Is Too Much Rubbish on the Web

So much variety of topics and content exists on the Web that it is impossible to see it all. The best approach is to check the most efficient Web sites that are maintained as general directories and are considered to be the best starting point for anyone exploring the Web. It is important to realize that there are various types of Web sites and pages developed by individuals, small businesses, large corporations, government agencies, and academic organizations. Most are considered by experts and analysts to be of relatively poor-quality and not very useful.

To businesses, the most interesting Web sites are those developed as marketing sites and customer service sites because such pages have the potential for developing additional business for the company. Numerous Web sites are also being developed providing shop fronts for merchants to rent, which relieves them from needing to acquire Web page development skills.

Numerous Web sites provide multimedia content materials and can be used as resources for design of multimedia Web pages. These provide advice and guidance on how to use Web development and navigation tools. USENET news groups also provide a continuous stream of information on the latest development on the Web and the Internet.

Beware of the Temptation

Some companies may want to get into the business of providing a product or service to those who want to exploit the Web. The opportunities appear to be endless, but so is the competition from many new ventures and well-established organizations. Business opportunities in this domain are limited to providing Web search and navigation tools, design or Web servers and access services, and design and implementation of Web home pages and multimedia content.

The hype surrounding all such Web-related businesses is to a large degree promoted by Wall street investors and new ventures that are issuing public stock. The most important point to remember is that most of those ventures are not profitable, and many stock issues are basically venture capital investors bailing out and taking their profits. Most Web browser firms that are giving products away are doing it on the assumption that a clientele will become hooked on the Internet and ask for more sophisticated products and services for which they will pay hefty charges. Whether or not this new business philosophy will prove to be correct still remains to be seen.

These business domains are already represented by numerous companies and a shakeout is already under way. For anyone contemplating that type of business, the best strategy probably involves judicious mergers and acquisitions of established ventures into more profitable entities. By the same token, the abundance of Web related services and products creates a buyers market, but companies availing themselves of such services must confirm the stability and financing of the vendors with whom they are dealing.

Honestly, Do You Really Need a Web Presence?

Whether or not a company needs a Web presence is highly questionable. Until it is possible to precisely measure the results and return on investment, most companies are taking a chance and may find that the investment was not worth the effort. On the other hand, the hype about the Web is such that it cannot be ignored, and in many instances, it has become a symbol of being technologically up-to-date.

Top management support and sufficient budgeting for all the aspects of Web presence planning, development, and maintenance are critical if a decision is made to proceed with such a project. The existing Web cyberspace should be searched for best competitive examples of Web home pages and a clear policy of Web outbound and inbound traffic should be established before work begins.

If the initial effort is confined to testing the waters, renting a Web server or sharing space on an existing server are the best strategies. Careful screening of available Web server presence suppliers is necessary to make sure that they meet access and throughput parameters, particularly if multimedia traffic is involved.

If a major effort to develop a Web presence for marketing reasons is made, the company should retain control of the Web server by building its own either with in-house resources or gaining assistance from a major consulting organization.

Network security is a major issue in developing a Web presence and a firewall must be set-up between the outside Web site and internal corporate networks to protect it from hackers, competitors, and spies.

Promotion of the Web site to lure customers to visit the site may become a major effort and should be budgeted upfront. It may include cross-linking with other Web sites, advertising, and public relations efforts along traditional lines in magazines, newspapers, radio, and TV.

Development of Web presence for companies, large and small, is a business opportunity for providers of Web search and navigation tools, Web servers and access services, and system integrators of Web sites with existing LANs and WANs. Despite rapidly growing demands in many market sectors, the field is already overcrowded and the choice of business partners should be carefully made.

Multimedia Connectivity Is Not Always What It Seems

Access to the Web through Internet Service Providers and online services varies widely from one type of service to another. The main issue facing a user is to select a service provider who offers access of sufficient bandwidth to transmit multimedia content to and from the Web with an acceptable speed and minimum latency or jitter. Keep in mind that not all Web connections are suitable for effective multimedia transmissions.

There are thousands of ISPs that offer connectivity with the Web on a local, regional, national, and international basis. Most major ISPs provide high-speed links, but many low-cost local ISPs offer only dial-up or ISDN access to the Web which is barely adequate for effective multimedia transactions.

Users must investigate ISPs independently to determine if their networks, Web servers, and connections to the Internet meet the requirements of proposed Web presence, multimedia content, and transmission parameters.

The questions to ask include Web access options, backbone topology, usage patterns, NAP connectivity, redundancy, Web server capabilities, Web hosting services, congestion, security provisions, utilization reporting, and pricing alternatives. Only a few ISPs provide global coverage and the most critical issue in international operations is to determine which ISP offers the most POPs in countries of importance to the user.

Get the Very Latest Web Browser Before Anything Else

The most important aspect of a Web browser is its ability to reproduce the Web server page on the user screen exactly as it was intended. Navigability of Web browsers and ease-of-use features are also important factors in selection of a browser. Other browser features becoming important are security aspects, caching of downloaded data and their subsequent manipulation. Other options depend on user background and preferences. For transmission of multimedia content, it is necessary to select Web browsers that can display images, graphics, audio and video clips within the browser window. Most browsers rely on external viewers for handling audio and video content. It is important to make sure that browsers used are configured to handle every multimedia file that is likely to be needed.

Get Agents, Spiders, and Robots to Do the Work

The concept of agents and search engines to relieve the tedium of searching the Web is very attractive if one can afford it. Agents are software programs that represent the user in interactive cyberspace and can operate across the Internet and within networks and databases as robots until their objectives are accomplished.

Agents are already being applied in such areas as discarding junk E-mail, network management, and searching large databases on the Web and the Internet. As a result, a new industry is developing with specialized companies developing new agent languages, operating systems, and applications. Intelligent agents also are being used to develop interactive multimedia online service networks that can handle users with various online and wireless devices.

But watch out. The activities of agents are similar in nature to those of a computer virus and there is also concern about responsibility and liability when agents misbehave and damage other agents or networking infrastructures.

A Multimedia Web Presence Is Quite an Effort

Development of a multimedia presence on the Web presents a considerable challenge to corporations. They must design, develop, and maintain home pages on a 24-hour basis to present an effective and competitive worldwide presence on the Web.

The home page, which is the first page of a Web site, must identify the corporation, describe its mission, products and services, and provide links to related pages with detailed background information, images, and other multimedia features.

The complexity of a Web site and the variety of linkages calls for advanced and careful planning with the support of top management. Storyboarding of the

Web site is the best approach which results in a flow chart of the site and facilitates logical development of the project.

Web pages are developed using HTML language and a company must either acquire the skills to use it or contract with a specialized service to develop its Web site and pages. Introduction of images, audio, and video into a Web site requires anchors associated with URL addresses of files which contain such multimedia content. Whether or not a user can receive multimedia content also depends on the configuration of the Web browser and multimedia capabilities of the PC platform in use.

Web sites must be placed on a Web server where 24-hour service and operation can be guaranteed. The Web site also must be announced to the Internet community to develop interest among users to visit it.

The design, development and maintenance of a Web presence is a major corporate undertaking. It should receive top management support, a sufficient budget, and a full-time Webmaster to assure its success.

Beware of the Many and Varied Web Development Tools

Web development tools depend on HTML language standards which apply equally to Web servers, browsers, and other editing tools. Because HTML standards are in constant flux, special care must be taken in selecting the latest Web site design tools to keep up with the most advanced Web environments.

The HTML editors on the market facilitate the process of creating Web pages. There are also HTML converter tools or filters for translating existing document formats to HTML without the need for HTML programming skills. But there is an overabundance of such tools on the Internet because many programmers create their own products and post them in expectation of developing business for themselves.

Several major Web page editing packages have gained prominence as popular design tools. These include Internet Assistant, HoTMetal, WebEdit, and others.

Other Internet protocols including FTP and Gopher are also worth considering as sources of HTML and other documents suitable for referencing them from the Web home pages.

Graphics and multimedia content imagemapping tools are among the most valuable in enhancing Web pages. This was a relatively complex process previously but imagemapping tools have simplified and popularized such pages. Creation of multimedia images and content for inclusion on Web pages remains a complex and difficult task.

Let Somebody Else Do All the Work

There are a large number of ventures that are positioning themselves to provide Web services that are likely to be in demand during the next few years. These include Web page, site, and server design and development, construction of firewalls, encryption of commercial transactions, tracking of Web site traffic demographics, interactive advertising, and electronic commerce cybermalls.

Corporations that do not possess the required skills or time to acquire such capabilities can pick and choose among those consultants who are increasingly operating in a buyers market. Nevertheless, companies facing extensive Web server development and maintenance are probably wise to develop comprehensive in-house skills for this purpose.

Web development services range from large system integrators and Internet access providers who can offer turnkey solutions to small consulting ventures specializing in one or two aspects of the business. Because Internet and Web access is expected to become a commodity, many small and marginal ISPs are developing Web design and maintenance consulting skills which they perceive as the mainstay of their future businesses. Outsourcing Web development is worth considering due to steep learning curves in acquiring the required skills and competitive pressures in the marketplace. Another important issue is the rapid change in Web development tools. Those who specialize in providing those services keep on top of those changes as a means of presenting the most competitive service.

Glossary

Access Defines the function of obtaining electronic entry into a disk, files, records or networks.

Access code A confidential combination of characters used for identification to gain access to a computer or network. Also known as password, user ID or name.

Address A unique code that identifies a network node.

ADSL *Asymmetrical Digital Subscriber Line*. This is a consumer telephone line whose bandwidth has been enhanced to T1 levels over 18,000 feet of copper wire lines that will provide video-on-demand services.

A/D *Analog to Digital conversion*. Usually refers to an A/D converter device which digitizes a continuous wave form analog signal into a digital bit stream. It includes the steps of sampling and quantizing.

Algorithm A sequence of processing steps that performs a particular operation, such as compressing a digital image.

Aliasing Undesirable visual effects in video usually caused by inadequate sampling. Jagged edges or curved object boundaries are the most common *(see artifacts)*. Anti-aliasing is software adjusting such effects.

Anchor A software tag designed to associate text with a hypertext link.

Animation Movement of an object on a screen from point-to-point (path) or displayed sequentially at specific time intervals (cycle).

ANSI *American National Standards Institute.*

API *Application Program Interface*. Formats of messages used to activate and interact with functions of another program.

APPN *Advanced Peer-to-Peer Networking.* A distributed client/server networking feature that IBM added to its Systems Network Architecture (SNA) designed to support efficient and transparent sharing of applications in a distributed computing environment.

Artifact An unnatural or unintended object observed in reproduction of an image in a video system.

ASIC *Application Specific Integrated Circuit.* A semicustom chip used in a specific application that is designed by integrating standard cells from a library.

ASCII *American Standard Code for Information Interchange.*

Aspect ratio The relative horizontal and vertical spacing of pixels on a display screen.

Asymmetric system A video storage and display system which requires more devices and processing to compress and store than to play back an image.

Asynchronous A method of transmission which does not require a common clock but separates fields of data by stop and start bits.

ATM *Asynchronous Transfer Mode.* A high-speed switching platform that can transmit voice, data, and video signals faster and more efficiently than traditional methods. It uses packets of fixed length of 53 bytes and is also known as BISDN or cell relay.

Audio Sound portion of a video signal or separate sound used to annotate objects on frames such as text, graphics, animation, and still images.

Audio buffer Computer memory segment or separate device for storage of audio data for playback associated with an individual frame.

Authoring language High-level programming language using natural English or mnemonics specifically designed for developing multimedia applications.

Authoring system A software product designed for users without programming skills for developing and testing multimedia applications.

Bandwidth The range of frequencies a given system is able to reproduce. The communications capacity of a transmission line or a specific path through a network measured in bits per second (bps). In a LAN bandwidth is analogous to throughput.

Base A software tag which defines the portion of a URL that is used in indirect addressing.

Baseband A network where the bandwidth is taken up by a single digital signal such as in Ethernet and Token-Ring LANs.

Baud A unit of speed defining the rate of transmission of binary data approximately equal to one bit per second (bps) at lower speeds. Common rates are 300, 1,200, 2,400, and 9,600 bps available from common carriers.

BISDN *Broadband Integrated Services Digital Network. (See ATM)*

Bitmap A sector of memory or storage which contains the pixels that represent an image arranged in the sequence in which they are scanned.

Bit-mapped graphic A graphic image that can be accessed on a bit-by-bit (pixel) basis and is directly addressable on the screen. These are typical in paint programs in which images are treated as collections of dots rather than shapes. Color bit-mapped graphics require several bits to describe a color in each pixel.

BLOB *Binary Large Object*. Defines very large data files such as those representative of multimedia which includes audio and video content.

Bookmark A feature of most Web browsers that allow the creation of a bookmark for Web pages of interest. As a result, these can be revisited directly by selection of a particular bookmark in the browser. Lists of bookmarks create the most interesting selections for a particular user.

Bridge A protocol independent hardware device with an interface for connecting or extending LANs of the same type or connecting LANs and WANs. Bridges can be transparent, translating or encapsulating types.

Broadband A network in which multiple signals can share the same bandwidth simultaneously through the use of multiplexing – splitting – the signal.

Browser A client navigation tool for the Web.

CAI *Computer-assisted Instruction (see CBT).*

CBT *Computer-based training.*

CCITT *Consultative Committee International Telephone and Telegraph.* An international body which develops standards for voice and video transmission and compression over common carrier and digital networks. *(See TSS)*

CDDI *Copper Distributed Data Interface.* An FDDI standard implemented on copper wires.

CD-I *Compact Disk-Interactive.* A multimedia delivery standard introduced by Philips and Sony targeted at consumer and education markets.

CD-ROM *Compact Disk-Read Only Memory.* An optical disk storage device with 680 MB capacity.

Cell relay see ATM and BISDN.

CGI *Common Gateway Interface.*

Chroma-keying Facility to replace selected colors on a video image with others that allow creation of different scenes against the background. Also known as color key.

Chrominance Signals of an image that represent color components such as hue and saturation. A black and white image has chrominance value of zero. Also known as chroma.

Circuit switching A switching method in which a dedicated path is set-up between the transmitter and receiver. The connection is transparent because switches do not attempt to interpret the data.

Clickable image Image on the Web page that the browser is monitoring for mouse input. Coordinates of a selected point are returned to the Web server for action.

Client A computer that remotely accesses the resources of a server in form of a processor or large memory systems. May also mean an application in a window system running on the same computer under a server process.

Client/server An architecture that distributes computing responsibility between a front-end and a back-end program. With two or more machines client/server can dramatically reduce network traffic and increase performance.

CMIP *Common Management Information Protocol.* A protocol developed by IBM and 3Com and endorsed by ISO that provides a specification and formats for collecting network management data as an alternative to SNMP.

Codec *Coder/decoder.* A special processor that can digitize analog audio and video signals and decode digital data back into analog form.

Common gateway interface The interface between programs that generate responses to client requests resident on the World Wide Web servers.

Compound document A document composed of a variety of data types and formats each derived from application that created it.

Compression The translation of video, audio or digital data singly or in combination to a more compact form for storage and transmission. Computer algorithms and other techniques are used to accomplish this compression process. *(See JPEG, MPEG)*

Concurrence Simultaneous transmission of or occurrence of two or more events or activities within the same time period.

Container A software tag for enclosing text with a start and end component.

Control track Component of a video signal, exclusive of picture and sound which provides essential synchronizing information.

Cyberspace Computer-generated electronic environment that is designed to give the user an artificial feeling of movement and discovery. *(See virtual reality)*

Data rate The speed of data transfer process normally expressed in bits per second (bps) or bytes per second (bps).

DCT *Discrete Cosine Transform.* A complex mathematical algorithm used in compression devices for eliminating redundant data in blocks of pixels on a screen. It is the basis for JPEG, MPEG, and CCITT compression standards.

Dial-up connectivity Availability of a connection between two devices through a phone line.

Digitizing The process of converting analog electronic signals into digital format that can be stored, manipulated, and displayed by a computer. It is accomplished by special A/D converters in form of Audio Capture Boards, Video Frame Grabbers, Scanners or combinations of those in a single circuit board.

Dissolve Gradual fading-out of an image on the screen as another appears.

Downlink Earth station used to receive signals from satellites.

Drop site A method of registering new Web pages consisting of a WWW page on which updates and additions to the links are listed.

DSP *Digital Signal Processor.* A specialized microchip designed to process efficiently digitized wave form data of sound and video. DSPs combine high speed of a microcontroller with the numeric capabilities of an array processor.

DVD *Digital Video Disk.* A new optical disk format with storage capacities up to 10 Gigabytes.

DVI *Digital Video Interactive.* This is a compression format for recording digital video on a CD-ROM disk that provides up to 72 minutes of full-motion video, four hours of 1/4 screen full-motion video or 14 hours of 1/8 screen full-motion video.

Editor A software program used for creating and modifying electronic content of files.

E-mail Electronic mail consisting of computer facility for sending and storing messages. E-mail can be sent to anyone with an Internet address but only users with MIME-compliant mail reader can receive text with various fonts images, audio, video, and other binary files.

Ethernet A commonly used LAN protocol standard that allows network nodes to transmit packets at any time over coaxial, twisted-pair, and fiberoptic cabling. Packet collisions resulting from such transmission freedom can delay a packet during transmission.

Fade A gradual change in brightness of an image or intensity of sound considered to be a special effect.

FAQ *Frequently Asked Question.* Documents with answers to frequently asked questions located in many parts of the Internet, particularly in newsgroups where they specify the ground rules for participation.

FDDI *Fiber Distributed Data Interface.* Standard developed by ANSI.

FDDI-Sync A variant of FDDI that provides priority to synchronous traffic on the LAN.

FDDI II A special new standard for isochronous LANs which carries traffic in channels instead of packets like FDDI.

Firewall A special gateway consisting of hardware and software between the internal network of an organization and the Internet. It protects the internal network from unauthorized access and potential damage by hackers.

Flame An E-mail message or comment in a newsgroup in response to some action that offended someone.

Flicker A phenomenon in a videodisk freeze frame when both video fields are not matched properly. A visible fluctuation of brightness of an image.

Forms HTML software tags that generate interactive Web pages. They can include buttons, text input areas, and menus.

Fps *Frames per second (See frame rate).*

Fractal *Fractional Dimensional.* Mathematical definition of a fractional element of an image after repeated application of a specific compression algorithm with theoretical compression ratio capability of 10,000:1.

Frame rate Speed at which frames are displayed on the monitor. Standard broadcast TV rate is 30 fps in North America, 25 fps in Europe. Minimum acceptable movement frame rate is 15 fps.

Frame A complete image in film or video consisting of two interlaced fields of 525 scan lines running at 30 frames per second (fps) in the NTSC system used in North America.

Frame grabber A digitizer that converts video images into digital data that can be manipulated by a computer program.

Freeware Software available without cost but without support.

FSIG *FDDI Synchronous Implementers Group* formed in December 1992, to expedite delivery of standardized distributed multimedia solutions to users.

FTP *File Transfer Protocol.* An Internet protocol and software used to transfer files between host computers. Web browsers generally contain all these commands and users do not have to be concerned about the details.

Full-motion video Display of video at the broadcast frame rate of 30 fps.

Gateway Interfaces designed to convert protocols between two different types of networks.

Gbps *Gigabits per second.*

Gigabyte (GB) Represents one billion bytes or 1,024 megabytes (MB).

Genlock *Synchronization generator lock.* Permits combination of two or more video sources by synchronizing their signals together to produce a recordable composite video that can contain elements from each source.

Gopher An Internet client/server protocol in the menu-based category that allows users access to files normally handled by a Web browser.

GUI *Graphical User Interface.* A screen interface with icons that allows direct manipulation of on-screen objects, menus, and dialog controls.

HDTV *High Definition Television.* A TV screen with resolution comparable to movie theater or 35 mm slide which requires at least 2 million pixels per frame. Standard NTSC TV resolution contains only 336,000 pixels.

Headend Facility in cable system from which all signals originate. It picks up local and distant TV stations and satellite programming and amplifies for retransmission through the system.

Heterogenous network A networks whose components represent several architectures.

Home page A Web location used as a virtual reception desk by a company with Web presence. Normally, the page includes a welcome greeting and list of alternative links to company information or services.

Horizontal rule A horizontal line used to divide sections of a document on a page.

Hotlist Used to record URL addresses of interesting Web locations usually in form of URL lists for clicking a rapid connection.

HTML *Hypertext Markup Language.* A set of codes added to plain text to indicate embedded images, links, hierarchical relationships, and other dependencies. HTML documents are interpreted by Web browsers and presented as multimedia screens with hyperlinks. HTML also allows the creation of enhancements to existing pages.

HTTP *Hypertext Transport Protocol.* The first part of an Internet address indicating to the Web browser existence of an HTML page.

Hypermedia Defines hypertext which contains a large percentage of multimedia content such as graphics, images, audio, and video.

Hypertext Linked pieces of text joined together in non-sequential manner and accessible by navigation through a series of menus.

Hypertext Markup Language Specialized document creating language for Web browsers.

Hypertext Transport Protocol Special Internet protocol for transferring documents and other data between systems forms the basis of the World Wide Web network.

H.261 ITU compression standard designed to facilitate the transmission of video images over digital networks at data rates ranging from 64 KBps to 2.048 MBps and also based on DCT algorithm. Also known as px64 Kbps standard, where p = 1,2,3...30 and intended primarily for videoconferencing and videotelephony.

Icon A small graphic symbol on a screen representing access to a program or specialized files and commands.

IMA *Interactive Multimedia Association.* An umbrella organization grouping over 230 suppliers and end-users to deal with multimedia standards and data exchange issues.

Intelligent hub A hardware device that provides linkage between various LANs and automatically accounts for new topology as changes and expansion take place.

Interactive An action that allows dialog between electronic content and the user.

Interactivity levels Pertains to interactive design features available with respective hardware configurations. Level One = consumer devices, Level Two = industrial devices, Level Three = all above interfaced with an external computer and peripherals. These do not relate to quality, values or sophistication of content and displays.

Interframe coding A video compression technique which concentrates on coding high-detail areas of a picture.

Intraframe coding A video compression technique in which half the picture information is eliminated by discarding every other frame and displaying each frame for twice the normal duration during playback.

Internet The largest internetworked system in the world consisting of a small number of high speed backbone networks, each linking thousands of smaller regional and local networks on a global basis.

Internet address Electronic address assigned to hosts using the TCP/IP protocol suite consisting of 32 bits.

IP address A unique number that identifies each host in a network.

ISDN *Integrated Services Digital Network.* A set of digital network interface standards consisting of a signaling channel and a number of 64 Kbps digital transmission channels that are used to provide circuit switched connections.

ISO *International Standards Organization.*

Isochronous A communications capability that delivers a signal at a specified, defined, rate desirable for continuous data such as voice and full-motion video.

ITV *Interactive television.*

JPEG *Joint Photographic Experts Group.* A standard for compression algorithms for digitizing still images based on DCT with compression ratios ranging from 10:1 to 80:1.

Kbps *Kilobits per second.*

Kilobyte (KB) Represents 1,024 bytes.

LAN *Local area network.*

Latency The state of being latent – present but not visible or active – applies to a power or quality that has not yet come into sight or action, but may at any time. Used to describe the delay in network transmissions of data.

Legacy system Mainframe and minicomputer-based information systems critical to *Fortune* 1000 corporations in running day-to-day operations. About 50% to 80% of MIS budgets are spent on maintenance of those systems.

Lossy A compression technique in which displayed and decompressed image does not contain all the original digitized data.

Lossless Any compression scheme that allows full recovery of original data.

Luminance Brightness values of all points in an image.

MAN *Metropolitan Area Network.* The name sometimes given to high-bandwidth networking facilities in a densely populated region such as a metropolitan area and its suburban business and institutional communities.

Mastering A real-time process in which videotaped materials are used to create a master optical disk which can be replicated into CD-ROMs.

Mbps *Megabits per second.*

MCI *Media Control Interface.* Platform-independent multimedia specification initiated by Microsoft in 1990, which provides a consistent way to control CD-ROM and video devices.

MCU *Multipoint Control Unit.* A device for bridging three or more videoconferencing users of the same or differing protocols.

MHEG *Multimedia and Hypermedia Experts Group.* An ISO activity concerned with coordinating specifications of multimedia design on any platform.

MIDI *Musical Instrument Digital Interface.* A series of digital bus standards for interfacing of digital musical instruments with computers.

MIME *Multipurpose Internet Mail Extensions.* A standard designed for exchanging multimedia E-mail and messages containing binary files, spreadsheets, programs, and databases.

MIPS *Million instructions per second.*

Modem Abbreviation for modulator/demodulator; provides a connection for transfer of data through telephone lines.

Mosaic A Web browser supporting HTML language that popularized the Web as an interactive Internet application with forms.

Mouse An input device that determines the location of the pointer on the screen.

MPC *Multimedia PC.* Minimum multimedia hardware delivery platform standard MPC-1 and MPC-2.

MPEG *Motion Picture Experts Group.* A standard for digital video compression which records only changes from frame-to-frame and is based on the DCT algorithm. Compression ratio is a trade-off between motion video quality, size of window, and frame rate.

Needs analysis A critical phase of the interactive multimedia design process based on the needs of the end-user.

Netiquette The informal set of rules for public behavior designed to police the Internet. Major rules include reading FAQs, avoid spamming, typing in lower case letters, and refrain from Internet abuse of any kind.

Network operating center A computer center dedicated to monitoring, control, troubleshooting, and user assistance on the network.

Newbie Any new user of the Internet.

Newsgroups Continuous, global discussion groups about every topic under the sun. Also known as Usenet or NETNEWS. Take the form of agglomerations of E-mail messages sorted by topics and distributed to thousands of users worldwide.

Node An addressable point in a network that can connect other peripheral devices and platforms to the network.

NTSC *National Television Standards Committee.* Defines North American color TV signal standards in 30 fps.

ODB *Object Database.* A database that can handle diverse and complex data including video, audio, bitmaps, graphics, animation, and unstructured text.

Online Connected interactively to the system and operational.

Operating system A suite of software routines that monitor the use of a system and supervise execution of application programs.

Packet switching Transfer of data by means of addressed packets or blocks of information. This differs from circuit switching because the network interprets some data and determines the routing during the transfer of a packet.

PAL Color TV signal format in Europe and some other countries. Uses interlaced scheme with 25 fps and 625 lines per screen.

Password A unique string of characters used as an identification code as a security measure to restrict access to interactive network systems and sensitive files.

Pixel *Picture Element.* The smallest element of a screen represented as a point of specific color and intensity level.

Platform Basic hardware technology of a computer system describing specific microprocessor and operating systems of a product.

Point-to-point protocol (PPP) The protocol that provides host-to-network and router-to-router connections over synchronous and asynchronous circuits.

Primitive A basic element for display such as a point, arc, line, circle, alphanumeric character or marker.

px64 same as H.261.

Quantizing The process of converting analog values into digital with a limited number of bits.

Radio button Represents one of several exclusive options that appears as a small circle and when selected shows a smaller circle inside.

RAM *Random access memory.*

Real-time The transfer of data that returns results so rapidly in actual time the process appears instantaneous to the user.

Resolution A measure of image quality of a display; refers to the number of pixels available on the display and controls the level of detail that can be presented.

RGB *Red Green Blue.* A color display signal consisting of separately controlled red, green, and blue beams which result in high-quality color output normally used in computer screens.

RIFF *Resource Interchange File Format.* Platform-independent multimedia specification developed by Microsoft in 1990, that allow audio, image, animation, and other multimedia elements to be stored in a common format.

RISC *Reduced Instruction Set Computer.* A computer processor set with simpler instructions but higher performance.

Router A hardware device that provides intelligent links between networks. Routers recognize protocols, addresses and compute the most effective route for data transmission.

Run-length coding A data compression technique that records repeated data elements with the same value and a count of the number of times they occur.

Sampling The process of reading and recording value levels of an analog signal at evenly spaced time intervals. It is a step in the process of digitization prior to encoding.

Sampling rate The rate at which sampling occurs during digitization. Audio digitizing may involve sampling of 16 bits of data at rates as high as 48,000 times per second.

Script A type of software program that includes a set of instructions expressed using specific rules and syntax combined with simple control structures.

SECAM *Sequential Couleur Avec Moniteur*. The standard for color TV developed in France, which is also used in Russia, Eastern Europe, and some other countries. It compares with PAL at 25 fps and the interlaced image is made up of 625 lines per frame.

Server A computer system with resources and large memory capacity that can be accessed and used by client machines.

Shareware Software that can be used for a period of time for evaluation and should be paid for if elected to be used permanently.

SLIP *Serial Line Interface Protocol*. A protocol that operates over telephone circuits or RS232 cables interconnecting two systems which being replaced by PPP.

Spamming Considered to be the abuse of E-mail when sending unsolicited advertising or promotional messages to large numbers of people on the Internet.

SMPTE *Society of Motion Pictures and Television Engineers*. The SMPTE time code is standard 8-digit code used in identification of frames in form of HH:MM:SS:FF (hours, minutes, seconds, frame numbers).

SNA *Systems Network Architecture*. An IBM network strategy that defines communications methods for many IBM systems ranging from PCs to mainframes. Introduced in 1974 it is supported by many vendors.

SNMP *Simple Network Management Protocol*. A popular protocol that provides specifications and formats for collecting network management data as an alternative to CMIP.

SONET *Synchronous Optical Network*. A new standard for transmitting a variety of light signals over optical fiber allowing different fiber systems to interconnect efficiently with an unprecedented level of accuracy and customer control. It includes a hierarchy of transmission rates ranging from 51.5 Mbps up to 2.4 Gbps at present.

Special effects Video image manipulation techniques for enhancing appearance. Includes effects such as dissolve, fade, wipe which are usually included as features in some video boards and authoring systems.

SQL *Structured Query Language.* The international standard for defining and accessing relational databases.

Storyboard Basic documentation of the proposed contents of a multimedia application, an advertising spot or film. Prepared screen-by-screen and includes information about types of video, audio, and other objects that will be used. May also include details of navigational objects and interactivity levels at each point of the application.

Synchronous traffic This type of transmission requires that a clock signal be transmitted with the data so both transmitter and receiver can agree on the time related bit location *(Compare to asynchronous).*

Tag This is a string of characters beginning with a < and ending with > used to mark-up text with specific display instructions.

TCP *Transport Control Protocol.* It provides reliable, connection-oriented, full-duplex data streams.

TCP/IP *Transport Control Protocol/Interface Protocol.* A protocol developed by the Department of Defense to connect dissimilar systems on a network commonly used in UNIX networks. It is also called the Internet protocol suite.

TIFF *Tag Image Format File.* A standard format used for scanning, storage, and interchange of gray-scale graphic images.

Timeout In an interactive system, it is the time limit within which a response must occur before a default branch of the program is executed automatically.

Token-Ring A LAN protocol standard requiring network nodes to receive the circulating token – the permission to transmit – before the node can transmit a packet. It is commonly found in IBM's SNA environments.

Touch screen Pressure sensitive display monitor often used as a multimedia control instead or in conjunction with a keyboard. The most sophisticated touch screens also include z-axis control which allows screen response at different rates depending on the level of pressure applied.

TSS *Telecommunications Standardization Sector.* Previously known as CCITT.

Tweening An animation technique where movement between key frames of a multimedia application is generated by the computer.

ULSI *Ultra Large Scale Integration.* Generally applies to memory microchips with over 1 MB storage capacity and comparable levels of integration for microprocessors and other circuits.

URL *Universal Resource Locator.* An address that includes the protocol to reference the data, the system, data paths, and filenames.

Uplink Earth station used for transmitting to satellites.

Usenet This is a worldwide network of UNIX systems used for E-mail and communications by special interest groups *(see Newsgroups).*

User account A basic record of information about a user stored in the system.

User ID A specific combination of letters and numbers that uniquely identifies a user to the system

VCR *Video Cassette Recorder.* Can be used with appropriate conversion device as input or output for multimedia applications. communications with remote party over existing networks or public telephone links.

Video-dial-tone New public services being introduced for transmitting video signals similar to audio telephony.

Videodisk An optical disk on which video signals have been recorded most often in NTSC analog format. Widely used as video input source for multimedia training applications.

Video for Windows Microsoft standard that allows end-users to view video within a window of their screen.

Video-on-demand Interactive TV concept for retrieval of video programs or movies from an interactive service at the consumer's convenience outside of conventional schedules.

Videotext Two-way interactive service using either cable or telephone links to connect a central computer to TV screens.

Viewer Software programs designed to output sound, images, and video from Web sites for specific MIME types of files.

Virtual Existing or resulting in an effect although without factual basis. A virtual device may exist in a computer memory only representing a hardware peripheral.

Virtual reality Also known as artificial reality, cyberspace, and telepresence. It is the use of computers to simulate real environments with which a user can interact.

VRML *Virtual Reality Markup Language.* The next generation markup language for the Web that relies on creating an environment for intuitive interaction rather than clicking on a page of text.

VTR *Videotape recorder.*

VUI *Video User Interface.* A next generation computing interface metaphor which will use a full-motion video window as part of the user interface and may employ icons to facilitate navigation.

WAIS *Wide Area Information Server.* A standard tool for indexing and text searching used with the Web.

WAN *Wide area network.* A network connecting technologically incompatible devices or LANs over long distances and typically using common carrier transmission facilities.

Web browser Client software for navigating and displaying Web pages.

Webmaster The person who is in charge for a particular Web page or site for a company.

Whiteboard A feature of multimedia conferencing that allows users at various locations using pointing devices to simultaneously edit, draw on, and annotate documents that include word processing, spreadsheets, graphics, engineering drawings, and video.

Wipe A special effect in which one image pushes aside another off the screen. Many different approaches exist.

World Wide Web The multimedia aspect of the Internet can be conceived as a revolutionary global publishing mechanism. It uses HTML as authoring language and http as the transport protocol and is supported by numerous client and server products.

WWW *World Wide Web.*

WYSIWYG *What You See Is What You Get.* A user interface of many authoring systems where the author sees the screens as he or she develops them exactly the way they will appear to the user.

Computer Technology Research Corp.

6 North Atlantic Wharf, Charleston, South Carolina 29401 U.S.A. • Tel: 803/853-6460; Fax: 803/853-7210

REPORT EVALUATION

Dear valued customer:

It is our continued desire and top priority to provide you with the most current and accurate computer technology information in our reports. Please assist us by taking a few minutes to answer the enclosed questionnaire. Your participation will help us to continue to provide professional service and quality reports to you. Please return the completed questionnaire by fax or mail. Feel free to attach additional sheets if you would like to add more comments. Your time and input are greatly appreciated.

Sincerely,

Edward R. Wagner

Edward R. Wagner
President

Report Title: ______________________________

Customer Name: ______________________________

Address/Phone: ______________________________

____

Rating System: 1=poor, 2=fair, 3=good, 4=above average, 5=outstanding	1	2	3	4	5
1. How would you rate your overall satisfaction with this report?	☐	☐	☐	☐	☐
2. How would you rate the informational content?	☐	☐	☐	☐	☐
3. How would you rate the technical content?	☐	☐	☐	☐	☐
4. Overall, how up-to-date is the report?	☐	☐	☐	☐	☐
How would you rate the quality of data provided regarding: a) product releases?	☐	☐	☐	☐	☐
b) price/performance data?	☐	☐	☐	☐	☐
c) product evaluations?	☐	☐	☐	☐	☐
d) management issues?	☐	☐	☐	☐	☐
5. How would you rate the quantity of illustrations?	☐	☐	☐	☐	☐
6. How would you rate the quality of illustrations?	☐	☐	☐	☐	☐
7. To what degree did this report provide the information which you were desiring to obtain on the subject matter?	☐	☐	☐	☐	☐

Continued on next page

Rating System: 1=poor, 2=fair, 3=good, 4=above average, 5=outstanding	1	2	3	4	5
8. How would you rate the readability of the report in terms of general appearance (type style, layout, etc.)?	☐	☐	☐	☐	☐
9. How would you rate the report's international coverage?	☐	☐	☐	☐	☐
10. To what extent will the material in this report figure into your decision-making?	☐	☐	☐	☐	☐
11. To what extent did you save time or money by reading this report? (Please explain briefly if possible)	☐	☐	☐	☐	☐

12. Is this the first CTR report you have purchased?	Yes ☐	No ☐
13. Would you purchase other CTR reports?	Yes ☐	No ☐
14. Would you recommend that other information technology professionals purchase this report?	Yes ☐	No ☐
15. Do you believe the information provided warrants the report's cost?	Yes ☐	No ☐
16. Were you satisfied with the service you received from our staff in fulfillment of your order?	Yes ☐	No ☐
17. Did your shipment arrive in good condition?	Yes ☐	No ☐
18. Were you satisfied with the delivery time of your shipment?	Yes ☐	No ☐

19. What additional information or topics would you have desired to see in this report that were not adequately covered?

20. What topics would you like to see us cover in future reports?

21. If you know of another individual whom you believe would be interested in receiving information concerning our report series, please list his/her full mailing address below:

Mail or fax your completed questionnaire to:

Computer Technology Research Corp.
6 North Atlantic Wharf
Charleston, SC 29401-2150 U.S.A.
Fax: (803) 853-7210

Thank you for your time and input!